The World's Most Dangerous Secret Societies

The Illuminati, Freemasons, Bilderberg Group, Knights Templar, The Jesuits, Skull And Bones And Others

James Jackson

Table of Contents

Introduction

Secret societies. To some, the name conjures up an image of a shadowy and elite cabal meeting behind smoke-filled rooms, discussing tactics of world domination and manipulation straight out of the most far-fetched espionage thriller. To others, the image of secluded men (and occasionally women!) banding together in exotic garb to perform colorful ceremonies and impart hidden knowledge and fancy but incomprehensible titles upon one another springs to mind. And to others, a fanciful and convoluted figment of the imagination sprung from only the most paranoid and incredulous minds is evoked by the title.

But just how far-fetched and fanciful is the prospect of a secret society? Could it be that there walks among us, in any given echelon of the population, groups given to exercise inordinate amounts of power and influence over the rest of us? Could these exotic members-only clubs really pose such an immediate threat to our well-being that our very way of life is endangered? At what point does the merely colorful, mysterious or deluded result in murder, mysterious deaths, unanswered disappearances, crime, extortion, control and in some cases, complete and unmitigated power?

The rationale and history behind secret societies have been amply covered in general works on the subject—some purely speculative, others works of wild conjecture, and even some which have been meticulously researched and documented. Yet few adequately demonstrate the effects of these groups on society at large. And with very good reason. A secret society, by its very definition, is a group that possesses secrets; either conducive to its internal doctrine or structure, wielded as a threat or even a reward to maintain control over its members, or resulting from clandestine activities that would present a clear and present harm to the world as a whole were they ever to be revealed. Yet this definition covers a whole range of groups and practices, from the relatively mild and harmless hazing practiced by thousands of college fraternities worldwide to organized crime cartels and even low-level street gangs. What is it about the secret society of popular legend and lore that continues to hold such appeal—and such danger—to countless individuals in their daily lives that differentiates these shadowy entities from their more visible counterparts?

More information—and subsequently, more deliberate *misinformation*—has been published in recent years than any time else. With the advent of the internet as a dominant means of communication, the costs and risks of revealing the tactics and methodology of formerly "arcane" organizations has diminished greatly. At any given time, the dedicated investigator can click on an infinite number of sites revealing a mind-bogglingly complex chain of associations that, more often than not, serve to confuse and bewilder all but the most steadfast of investigators.

Some have been adequately revealed as hoaxes—the 19th Century fraud instigated by Leo Taxil regarding the elusive "Order of the Palladium" springs to mind. Others are altogether figments of urban legend that have resulted in a series of bizarre coincidences and tortuous links—the supposed "Four Pi Movement" alluded to by Maury Terry in his bestselling book *The Ultimate Evil* is one such prominent example. Yet still others have been so adequately researched, so ably presented, and whose coincidences are so improbable that one cannot help but put full faith in the veracity of at least *some* of these claims. Perhaps separating the fact from the fancy is one of the biggest dilemmas in adequately chronicling the danger of a secret society. And perhaps, that is but one of the goals of their effective operation.

Fear of repercussion is at the core of the concealment and mysteries of a secret society. And with good cause. Many of these groups hold basis in ideological tenets that are not only firmly accepted by popular convention, but in some cases, diametrically *opposed* to it—tenets that in not so distant times, were punishable by persecution and even death. In our more skeptical, materially driven times, we are given to take the world of appearances solely at face value, as ipso facto. We neglect to remember that for many of our ancestors, the world of appearances—the phenomenological world as we know it—was an allegory that alluded to much deeper, almost incomprehensibly profound truths that shaped our thinking in radical ways. This link is at the heart of the often-quoted Hermetic aphorism: "As above, so below." Flying as it did in the face of official Church and State-ruled forms of discourse, adherents could risk the most dire forms of persecution merely for venturing these views, and subsequently had to work under the mantle of strict secrecy, being driven underground in the face of reformations and inquisitions where they fermented, often forging links with one another and developing a highly dubious and complex lore.

Yet scoff as we may at such unsophisticated, "mystical" forms of magical thinking, we neglect to remember that many of its adherents went on to influence the world in dramatic ways. The Greek philosopher Pythagoras, who is credited with introducing geometric theorems into the world, was one such member of a "mystery school"—indeed, a secret society where revelation of secrets was punishable by death. The Elizabethan scholar, magician, and court astrologer to Queen Elizabeth I, John Dee was one such proponent of Hermetic thought, and his advice to Queen Elizabeth regarding the invasion of the Spanish Armada in 1588 is largely why English is the dominant language in North America. Many of the leading ideologues and artists of the Italian Renaissance were profoundly influenced by Hermetic themes; and even the noted father of scientific rationalism and "father of Enlightenment" Sir Isaac Newton had a long-standing interest in Hermetic and Alchemical treatises. And the Masonic involvement of such U.S. founding fathers as Paul Revere, George Washington and Ben Franklin has been sufficiently documented elsewhere. Are we to hold these tenets, as far-fetched and superstitious as they may seem, to be bygone relics of a distant and unenlightened era? Or has their influence on world history been actually more prevalent than appearances lead one to believe?

Yet, fears of repercussion can lead to more legitimate, even *sinister* concerns than merely unpopular or superstitious belief. Is the very clandestine nature of such organizations masking intents that are detrimental to the well-being of society as a whole? Has their infiltration into every sector of political thought and action become so widespread that they are an entrenched, if subterranean, part of our current world structure? Are their agendas borne out of domination and the need for revenge? Do their actions compromise the integrity of any free-thinking and upstanding social mechanism? In a time in which public discourse allows for the open (if critical) exchange of ideas and thoughts, what is so dangerous that members conceal their identity in dire oaths of secrecy? In short, what are these societies trying to hide?

The fact is, the trails of these societies can lead to some disturbing associations and occurrences and paint a much more damning picture than mere unconvention. Tales of murder, crime, political intrigue and conspiracy are so prevalent that merely painting them as purveyors of an unsophisticated belief system is to betray the very dangers that they pose. Some of the most seemingly innocuous and benign organizations—such as the Society of Jesuits—spin a much more dire and noxious web of deceit than you would ever think to imagine upon critical examination, as you will soon find out.

One reason for the continued allure of secret societies lays in the very exclusivity their secrecy engenders. No longer misguided believers in illogical mumbo-jumbo, members are holders of "forbidden" knowledge sternly safeguarded from the prying eyes of profane and critical non-believers. No longer mere citizens, by dint of their immersion in a subterranean world of exotic and ritualized customs, members become possessed of power and influence unimaginable to their merely mortal neighbors. Even at a time in which the rapid and unconstrained transmission of information threatens the very security of such formerly hidden membership and "knowledge," the true believer takes it upon his or her self for granted that the traditions of deceit and concealment they choose to partake in is inviolable and beyond reproach. The question is for how long?

 While preparing for the research in this book, it struck me that two distinct classifications could be made for distinguishing a secret society. The first would be the more visible, or *overt* secret society. Generally speaking, these are organizations which maintain a highly visible public profile, accessible by means of phone book, internet or even highly publicized physical appearances. These organizations frequently solicit or court membership, assuring the would-be candidate that their very openness, visibility and culpability should be sufficient insurance against nefarious and fraudulent intentions, instead insisting either that there are "no secrets" or sometimes even half-mockingly referring to such "supposed" secrets as largely irrelevant traditions—bygone remnants of a much earlier time holding no greater power than a deferral to routine. The would-be candidate is then lulled into a sense of security and relaxation—"Surely, *these* guys must not be hiding anything since they're willing to take the time to talk to little old me."

One such glaring example of an *overt* secret society is Freemasonry. Masquerading under the guise of benevolent philanthropy and civic duty, members are now widely viewed as little more than a charitable social club cloaked in colorful costume and ritual, one whose membership numbers are slowly dwindling due to decreased interest among younger generations. And for all ostensible purposes, at your local Masonic Lodge level, that's likely to be the case; so much so, that in many regions of the U.S., Freemasonry has had to launch a highly visible public relations campaign to ensure its continued interest and survival.

Yet throughout history, upper echelon members have been implicated in every sort of conspiratorial undertaking imaginable—from spying to assassination, from bribery to infiltration sowing the seeds of political unrest and rebellion. This isn't to imply that your friendly uncle—whose father's father was in the Masons and his father's father before that—is guilty of undertaking political subterfuge and extortion. But if these facts were made available to the general public, would there be such a strident need to attach the historically important faces of Benjamin Franklin and Harry Truman to their much maligned name?

Oftentimes, the *overt* secret society will make claims of an unfounded historical lineage or go through dire efforts to conceal questionable past histories. Members are made to swear great and unyielding oaths to hold the secrets of that organization in strictest confidence, ensuring that their revelation will be met with a suitable and dramatic fate merely hinted at by the outlines of that somber oath. An unspoken climate of fear emerges in the secret society, imbuing it with all the hallowed ethos of sanctity and vigilance to be found in the most unbridled religious zealotry (it is worth noting that in the *overt* secret society, implied religious and philosophical devotion is nominally considered *a priori* fact, as opposed to the *covert* secret society which is considerably more political and influential in scope. Occasionally, overlappings can occur, such as the relationship between the Skull & Bones society—a perfectly prominent example of a *covert* secret society—and the aforementioned example of Freemasonry.) Even when not outwardly religious in scope—such as in the cases of the Jesuits or Opus Dei—this aura of divine safeguarding and sanctimony has led to the cultish appeal of the society, in particular for those true believers who are disaffected from, or otherwise non-adherents of, conventional religion. The substitution of the secret for the sect thereby takes the place of a sort of divine revelation for the true believer what may be a curious method of transubstantiation, indeed.

The other classification is that of the clandestine, or *covert* secret society. Unlike the *overt* society, no attempts at public outreach are made on behalf of the *covert* one. Public admission is *not* possible, except by invitation only—and, to quote a now clichéd precept, "If you have to ask, you'll never know." Reasons for this hermetically guarded level of secrecy may vary from organization to organization, but generally one thing in common is that their interests generally extend to widespread global geopolitical infiltration and influence, and at times, highly organized and systemic criminal and terrorist organizations. The secrecy of the *covert* society is not motivated by tradition or even influence over lower-level members, but *necessity*. Both the much dreaded spectre of the Illuminati and the vow of silence practiced by the *La Cosa Nostra* syndicate are glaring examples of the occult operations of a *covert* secret society.

Other times, the revelation of the *covert* society's existence could cause so much damage to well-established institutions—such as the

Priory of Sion or the Bilderberg Group—that their very foundations could crumble, a moment such groups may indeed be hoping to seize upon. Instead, they bide their time, weaving their way into a highly complex web of intrigue and legend, fact and fiction, both insisting upon their non-existence and alternately placing public reminders of their "alleged existence" in such a way that the idle observer is caught up in a wave of subterfuge and confusion.

One such glaring example of this misinformation campaign was the COINTELPRO operation directed by the FBI under Director J. Edgar Hoover between the mid 1950s and early 1970s which aimed at surveying, infiltrating, discrediting and disrupting domestic political organizations that allegedly posed a threat to "national security, and existing social and political order" and was explicitly denied by the organization and its director until official documentation of the program was exposed and made public in 1971, prompting an official investigation into its tactics.

Leadership in *covert* societies are sometimes hereditary, being passed down in generational lines akin to monarchism—the reinstitution of which is, in fact, an alleged goal of some of these cliques. Other times, a feigned leadership has been attributed to noted historical and cultural figures through an elaborate campaign of misinformation and well-constructed lore, granting a lineal if seemingly improbable succession of historical validity to the machinations of a society.

When attempting to endeavor a work of this scope, it's important to take into consideration all sources, no matter how outlandish they may seem. Inevitably, one comes to classify these sources under one of three potential categories I will dub the three "S"s: the speculative, the spurious and the skeptical. As the adage says, where there's smoke, there's often fire. The speculative helps enable a critical and subjective eye towards the potential veracity of claims, ensuring both detachment and an open eye towards viewing possible connections. The spurious—often the result of tenuous connections and credulity towards unsubstantiated accounts—can often reveal hidden aspects that you had never in your wildest dreams thought possible, and aspects that upon closer examination reveal a definite claim towards historical validity. It is in the realm of the skeptical that we are confronted with a whole new dilemma, however. Unwilling to entertain the possibility that the vast web of intrigue and deceit is much vaster than his understanding allows it to be, the skeptic casts doubt upon anything that does not conform into his or her preset conclusions. His bias becomes all too apparent and unbending in its stubborn refusal of anything that doesn't remotely connect to its predisposed parameters—and sometimes, his or her own vested interests. In this book, I have strived to separate legend from reality, fact from fiction, and examine how both seemingly opposite sides can be weaved into a highly complex series of associations, and ones that can often influence one another in the most unexpected ways. It is likely that some readers will see aspects of all three "S"s throughout the book. The most I can ask for is an open mind.

It is also likely that some readers, particularly younger ones, will find material that has been well recounted elsewhere. I mentioned younger ones specifically because, having been brought up under the auspices of the information age, they've had a wider berth of both information as well as misinformation to absorb, reflect and mull over. Younger ones also seem more conducive to the act of critical thinking and incredulity to firmly established disavowals of the existence of these groups from conventional quarters, something which as time passes grows more and more assailable. I'm grateful for the open minds and quick wits I see from younger generations, and encourage them solely to draw their own conclusions—as much as I would any other generation. I can only hope this work will help encourage you to do so, regardless of your age.

This work is meant as both introductory and cautionary. I do not intend it to be the final say on the matter of secret societies, my own or anyone else's; far from it, I believe that as more information is made readily available to the general public, the need for more specialized works will be in higher demand. It is not intended to promote fear or prejudice, but to instill vigilance and critical thought towards established narratives of both history and legend. The truth may indeed be the strongest sword of all. And if I have done anything to sharpen that sword, then my task is complete.

Chapter One: THE HASHSHASHINS

Alamut. There isn't much bustle these days in this fertile valley nestled among the Elburz mountain range of northern Iran, overlooking the capital city of Tehran. Nestled as it is by the province of Qazvin—known for its history as a center of trade, calligraphy and culture—to the south, and the Mazandaran province—known for its forests, bridges and as the birthplace of the last shah of Iran—to the north, it's as if the region is frozen in time. Sure, there are slightly more modern roads that steer through here, curving through the imposing crags, gullies and hills; but even these seem foreboding in comparison to the densely huddled villages you leave as you make your ascent through the vastly impenetrable boulders and hills. Even the rivers, ravines and lakes seem to hum more like a funeral chant than a natural, gurgling stream. The preternatural silence that crowns these stones, punctuated by the occasional lone cry of an eagle, is less a welcome solace than an omen warning to the unwary visitor that there are secrets drenched in blood and viscera buried deep within the ruins and rubble. Frozen in time, the first impression you get upon taking in the surrounding mountains and boulders is that not very much has changed since the early 12th century. And for all ostensible purposes, it hasn't. After all, bones have their secrets to keep as well.

It's perhaps ironic that we begin our review of secret societies at what has been popularly dubbed the very cradle of civilization. Perhaps not so ironic, after all. Perhaps secrecy is fundamental to the human condition. And perhaps the whole of the collective human experience as we know it is marked to some degree by the twin hands of manipulation and bloodshed. Cain and Abel. Master and servant. Tyrant and subject. Perhaps when we learn how deeply ingrained these processes are within us, we can begin to see them as obsolete mechanisms that have far outlived their usefulness. Distant relics of an unfortunate past. As distant as—Alamut.

Though the time of the Hashashins is long past, their relevance is still integral to our study. Though the last of the Hashashins died over six hundred years ago, their presence still lives on to this day, embodied in modern terrorist organizations, rogue mercenaries and military juntas—embodied in the very heart, brains and sinews of anyone who would seek to control, dominate and tyrannize through the means of force, bloodshed and menace to pursue *any* political, religious or economic agenda, regardless of faction or sect. In fact, their very name lives on to this day, entered into everyday language: *assassin*.

And without a thorough knowledge of the origin of the tactics secret societies have developed throughout history, those who refuse to remember the past are condemned to repeat it.

Origins of the Hashashin

Perhaps the blueprint for all secret societies, an understanding of the role the Hashashin played is impossible without understanding the context in which they developed. By the 12th century, Islam had splintered into several distinct branches, two of whom are still locked in a bitter conflict to this day: The Shia and the Sunni. The Sunni, who represent the largest denomination of Muslims in the world, maintain that Abu Bakr, the father-in-law of the prophet Muhammad, is the first and rightful caliph—the direct political and religious successor to the prophet—of the Muslim community. In distinction, Shi'ite philosophy declares that the prophet's son-in-law and cousin Ali holds rightful claim to the title of caliph. Within this divide, numerous sub-divisions occur, each claiming distinct lineages and successions as varied and conflicting as their tenets. Within the Shi'ite branch, the three largest subdivisions are recognized as the Imamiyyah, the Ismaili, and the Zaidi.

There is not enough space to detail the specific differences between various branches and divisions of faith. Suffice to say, that by 1090, much of the Middle East was largely under the rule of the Fatimid Caliphate, who claimed direct origin from Fatima, the first daughter of the Prophet. The caliphate itself was explicitly Shi'ite in scope, with the vast majority of rulers being adherents of Ismailism. One of the most visible branches of Ismailism at that time was the Nizari branch, which flourished throughout Persia and Syria in the 11th Century. And it is directly to the Nizari branch that the Hashashin developed and flourished, under the stern and all-watching leadership of its founder and visionary, Hassan-i-Sabbah.

The Old Man of the Mountains

There is no accurate date or records for the birth of Hassan-i-Sabbah, and what little we know about his upbringing and early life stems from an allegedly autobiographical account quoted in the anonymously penned Ismaili chronicle *Sarguzasht-e Sayyidnā*. The account states that Hassan was born in Persia in the 1050s to a Imamiyi family, and was raised with the tenets of that faith in the city of Rey, where the future Grandmaster also studied alchemy, philosophy, astronomy—and it is rumored, certain occult doctrines practiced by renegade Muslim imams.

Rey was home to a burgeoning movement of Ismaili missionaries, and the young Hassan was converted to the doctrine at the age of 17, eventually swearing allegiance that same year to the Fatimid Caliphate in Cairo. It was in Cairo that Hassan studied in-depth with leading missionaries and clerics of Ismailism, eventually earning a reputation as one of the most fervent and devoted disciples of the Ismaili creed. Accounts vary as to his journeys from the age of 17 until his return to Persia in 1081. Was he imprisoned? Persecuted? One account tells of Hassan's meetings with a group of heterodox Muslims in Syria, where he was trained in the principles of magic and sorcery. One thing is for certain; upon his return, Hassan settled within the Elburz mountain range where, after establishing several Ismaili communities, he drew the ire of Nizam-al-Mulk, grand vizier of the Seljuq empire, prompting his retreat deep into the mountains of Alamut in 1088.

It was at Alamut in 1090 that Hassan formulated his grand strategy; to formulate a clandestine army and religious order of *fedayin* (in Arabic, literally 'the Men who accept Death') devoted to the expansion of the Nizari Ismaili creed, structured in a hierarchal and initiatory structure. Hassan served as the secretive and omniscient Grandmaster of the order for 35 years until his death in 1124, during which time it is said he only left his quarters twice to observe from his impenetrably constructed fortress (known as 'the Eagle's Nest') the heavens from its rooftop.

Below the Grandmaster served several of his trusted chiefs and strategists known as the Grand Propagandists, charged with disseminating the Grandmaster's orders; beneath these, served the Propagandists, who were charged with recruiting men from outlying villages into both the Nizari Ismaili creed and, should their devotion be loyal enough, the Order itself; the Rafiqs, or companions of the Order; and finally, the Lasiqs, or adherents themselves. It is from the Lasiqs that the Grand Propagandists personally elected to train in order to become the most feared and reviled assassins of their times, targeting not only rival Muslim sects (including the Sunni Seljuq empire, who were all but decimated by Hassan and his Order, who swore an oath to revenge the Grandmaster's persecution,) but also invading Christians and allies during the First Crusade (it is worth noting that there is strong evidence that the Hashashin made direct contact with the Knights Templar, of whom we will discuss in the following chapter.)

Each convert to the Order was expected to go through a series of nine initiatory degrees. In the first, the pupil was thrown into a state of confusion, through analogy and teaching, towards the tenets of his previous religious and political convictions. This is the source of the maxim "Nothing is True, All is Permitted" often attributed to Hassan (although there is no documentation stating that Hassan uttered these words, its popularization is largely due to the writings of countercultural icon WIlliam S. Burroughs.) At this point, the pupil was so disoriented by the dissection of his beliefs that he had no point but to submit to the blind obedience of his teacher.

In the second, he was taught that God's approval cannot be won except through the allegiance to his imam, or teacher, viewed as the guardian of God's word. In the third, he is instructed into the nature of his imam. In the fourth he is taught that Mohammed was not the last of the Prophets, and that the Qur'an is not God's final revelation to man—an implicit breach with the teachings of the Qur'an. The fifth and sixth elaborate on the allegorical nature of the outward practices and customs of Islam. The seventh held that both humanity and creation were one, with all phenomena existing as a fraction of the whole, including both creative and destructive power. The eighth taught that all religion and ideology was fraudulent—including Islam; preparing the initiate for the ninth and final secret: that the student was now freed from belief, acting as a purified philosopher in the knowledge that "nothing" literally *was* true, and that the only permissible "belief" was *action*, and furthermore that the only possessor of the reasons for carrying out any action whatsoever was the mysterious Grandmaster of the Order—Hassan-i-Sabbah himself.

How were so many impressionable young men so easily swayed to renounce their upbringing and the beliefs of conventional Islam and plunge headfirst into nihilism and martyrdom for the sake of one man's lust for omnipotence and revenge?

Deep within the maze-like fortress of Alamut, Hassan had constructed a lavish artificial paradise, replete with beautiful gardens, music, flowing rivers and ravishing dancing houris to bedazzle the eyes of would-be converts, unwittingly drugged with liberal amounts of hashish (from where the Order derived their namesake.) With his Propagandists leading them through a tour of this paradise, the pilgrims either became so entranced by the visions before them that they converted on the spot, begging to while away their time in this Eden; or became so frightened that they begged to flee, swearing that their hosts must be sorcerers or magicians. In either case, it was only through obedience to divine will of Hassan-i-Sabbah that entrance or exit was permitted. Only by swearing their fealty to this mysterious Master were these senseless young men granted access to paradise on earth; or return to their former lives. Few refused.

And how successful was this tactic, which marks the first historical instance of brainwashing?

The influence of Hassan swept not only through Persia, but Egypt, Syria, Azerbaijan and much of the Arab world—rumored to reach as far as France. Acting upon the Grandmaster's orders, his faithful *fedayin* gained entrance into courts, villages and camps, often disguised in local garb and speaking in local dialects. After gaining the trust of those rivals they were ordered to infiltrate, they assassinated each target by dagger, always in full public view and always in daylight (it is worth noting that the Hashishin were never permitted to murder a civilian.) Their first target was Hassan's old rival, Nizam-al-Mulk. Their network of fear and stealth soon spread throughout Persia and Syria, with hundreds—perhaps thousands—of assassinations being committed before the eyes of a quivering public, who no longer knew which stranger to trust. Nor did neither the Order nor their campaign of terror end with the death of Hassan-i-Sabbah. Over time, new Grandmasters were selected, each swearing to uphold the legacy begun by this mysterious Old Man of the Mountains. Countless regions and properties were brought under their command. Crusading knights spun endless tales regarding their ruthless and mercenary foes, giving rise to the eventual adoption and latinization of the term, "assassin." And then—it came to a halt.

The fall of the Hashishin empire came about with a Mongol attack at Alamut in 1256. Their fortress and paradise, seized. Their spirits and numbers, diminished substantially. The few remaining members spread out into Syria, where they acted as mercenaries for hire by local sultans and emirs. There is some speculation that they continued their teachings and practices well into the fourteenth and perhaps even early fifteenth centuries. And there is even some speculation that the influence of their internal teachings lives on to this very day, embodied in certain sects of the Iranian Mandaean faith and Kurdish Yezidi religion. But the prestige that the Hashishin enjoyed for almost two hundred years is now a fleeting memory. Or is it?

Legacy of the Hashishin

As stated earlier, the Hashishin fell in the thirteenth century, yet their ethos of carnage and terror continues to this day. It was felt in the Duvalier regime of the 1960s and 1970s with the secret police of his elite Tonton Macoute corps. It was in the killing fields of Cambodia of Pol Pot's Khmer Rouge party and the unspoken corpses that lay buried in Chile as a result of the Pinochet administration. And it is embodied in the more recent brutalities committed worldwide by such outfits as Al Qaeda, the Islamic State and Boko Haram. It is not exclusive to Islam—by and large, a peaceful religion—and claims allegiance to neither sect nor country. It is in the hearts of those who willingly perpetrate evil under the guise of an ulterior agenda; and therein lays its strength. It is perhaps, the *ultimate secret* of any secret society. Power. At any given cost.

Chapter Two: THE KNIGHTS TEMPLAR

Perhaps no other secret society is enjoying a greater resurgence in popularity currently than the Order of the Knights Templar. From Dan Brown's best-selling novel *the Da Vinci Code* to countless Hollywood blockbusters, numerous theories and speculation surrounds this pre-Medieval phenomena, and it's easy to see why. With their colorful hybrid of valiant chivalry, unanswered mysteries and unmitigated bravado, the historical Knights Templar cut a broad swath through the collective unconscious, at once evoking the gallantry of the Crusades, the exotic mystique of journeys into foreign lands and pathos for their ultimate demise. Apologists for the Knights Templar portray them as misunderstood martyrs, whose self-sacrifice at the behest of imperial conquest forever altered the course of history. Hardly a bad reputation for an order that was disbanded and burned at the stake over seven hundred years ago.

Yet the Templar mystique has continued to filter, often times unseen, not only into popular lore but through the underground stream of secret societies. In this chapter, I hope to examine not only the history of the order as well as their mysteries, but their influence in more shadowy undertakings as well. An influence that may indicate not only the undying love for the Templar mystique and the continuation of their ideals, but perhaps a continuation of their very existence itself.

Origins of the Knights Templar

The Poor-Fellow Soldiers of Christ and of the Temple of Solomon, more commonly referred to as the Knights Templar, came about in 1120 at the urging of French knight Hugues de Payens, who had approached both the King and Patriarch of Jerusalem to grant an official monastic Order for the protection of pilgrims visiting the Holy City of Jerusalem. At the time of their inception, the Templars only numbered nine in their ranks, all of whom had sworn a specific vow of poverty. Just thirty years later, their numbers had swollen to the thousands and were prosperous enough to lend money and credit to both citizens and government figures alike.

During the time of the Crusades, the Templars were often a key military component for the expansion of the Holy Roman Empire, being utilized as advanced shock troops in some of the most decisive battles of the conquest— including the battle of Montgisard, where some

500 knights helped defeat the legendary sultan Saladin's troops, which numbered over 26,000 combatants. Both their reputation as fearless and feckless warrior-monks as well as the uncouth lore surrounding them (a regular euphemism of the time was "to drink and swear like a Templar") helped establish the reputation of the Knights Templar as one of the most elite and fearsome scourges to attack the Middle East; a reputation they shared with the Hashishins of the previous chapter (of whom, the Templars undoubtedly came into contact with, and it is rumored, integrated certain philosophical tenets and mysteries into their secret initiation rites.)

By 1307, both the wealth, reputation and arrogance of the Templars had fallen into negative favor, particularly with the newly elected Pope Clement V (who sought to merge the order with another Christian military council, the Order of the Hospitallers, granting him benefit and power over both) as well as King Philip IV of France (who was in debt to the Templars as a result of his war with England.) Rumors began to abound about the Templars "secret" teachings; they were reputed to regularly engage in homosexuality, both denying the divinity of Christ and both trampling and spitting on the cross as part of their initiation rites, and worshipping a strange "bearded" idol of a head (alternately, the head of a goat) they referred to as "Baphomet."

These charges, along with others that constitute what was unquestionably heretical in 14th century France, have never been proven. But they have also never been *disproven.* Homosexuality has been a common practice among soldiers who, traveling long distances of many years without wives, seek some form of gratification, and may have been more prevalent among warrior-monks sworn to uphold a vow of celibacy. Denying and insulting the divinity of Jesus may seem like an unusual practice among sworn defenders of Christendom; but what better way to instill fear and test a potential recruits' bravado than attacking the general tenets of their sworn allegiance?

Numerous theories abound for the presence of Baphomet. These include, a linguistic corruption of the prophet Muhammed, or Mahomet; a symbol of the "baptism of wisdom" (the direct translation of the Greek term "baphe-metis"); and a literal idol (it is interesting to note that in cabalistic theory, the lesser countenance of God—the "Zaur Anpin"—is revealed as a human head.) Regardless of these elaborations, one thing is certain. On Friday, October 13th of 1307 (the origin of the superstition of Friday the 13th), King Philip ordered the arrest of several hundred Knights Templar, including their grandmaster Jacques de Molay, and formally charged them with heresy, financial corruption, bribery and secrecy. Their assets were seized, members were tortured and burned alive at the stake (including de Molay) and the order was formally dissolved. The few Templars who survived the extermination went underground into recluse, reemerging a few years later to forge alliances with other military Christian orders prevalent in Europe at the time, such as the Order of Teutonic Knights and the Knights of St. John.

The Templars may have died in the most ignominious of manners. But their legacy—and some say their secret teachings—continue to this day. Sometimes in the most sinister form imaginable, as you will soon see.

The Legacy of the Templars

The Templar mystique continues to this day, permeated through the teachings of esoteric orders and secret societies as well as seemingly innocuous entities. The international youth organization Order of de Molay (a Freemasonic offshoot), professing to teach young men to become better and more responsible community leaders and organizers, takes its name from the "martyred" Templar, Jacques de Molay. The Catholic fraternal organization the Knights of Columbus freely admit that their structure is modeled after the spirit of the Knights Templar. And the French Revolution—widely held to be masterminded by the Order of Illuminati (of whom we'll go into detail in subsequent chapters—found an unlikely ally in the Templars when, during the public execution of Louis XV, an unknown man lept onto the scaffolding to yell, "Jacques de Molay, thou art avenged!" before the applauding crowd before disappearing back into mystery. A blood-drunk boast? Or a Templar descendant?

Freemasonry and the Knights Templar

Certain traditions hold that some surviving Templars—who were widespread in their travels and most certainly held alliances and links with numerous European countries—went on to the British Isles (in particular Scotland) where they perpetuated their teachings and practices in secret, eventually forming the nucleus of one of the most powerful and influential secret societies in the West: the Ancient and Accepted Rite of Freemasonry.

The link between the Templars and Freemasonry became even more brazen in the 18th century when the High Knights Templar of Ireland Lodge accepted a charter from the Mother Lodge of Freemasonry in Ireland (itself said to be received from a reconstituted Templar order in Paris) establishing and recognizing their claims of Masonic jurisdiction, eventually incorporating their rites into what has been known as York Rite Masonry.

This rite is only available by invitation only, and ostensibly, only Freemasons who profess belief in Christianity (as opposed to standard Freemasonry which is available to anyone who professes belief in a higher power of any sort) are eligible. Yet the historical Knights Templar, who were also a nominally "Christian" organization, were alleged to hold beliefs diametrically opposite to conventional Christian doctrine, including the rejection of Jesus Christ (perhaps influenced by contact with the nearby heretical Cathar sect of Gnostics active in the 12th and 13th centuries in the region.) Could it be that their Masonic descendants also teach similar doctrines in their lodge meetings?   Doctrines hidden, even from the eyes of the sincere but misguided new recruit?

The Priory of Sion

Exposed in the early 1980s by writers Michael Baigent, Richard Leigh and Henry Lincoln in their best-selling *Holy Blood Holy Grail*, the Priory of Sion fulfills the ultimate archetype of a secret society: a hereditary, and generational group of French monied elite who claim a lineage directly back to the Knights Templar guarding a central and highly damaging secret. A secret so damning, it could bring down the foundations of Christianity itself. Namely, the Priory of Sion holds that Jesus did not die on the cross, but survived; and furthermore, established a bloodline with the otherwise vilified Mary Magdalen that formed both the Merovingian dynasty, and through successive generations, the Templars themselves. They purport that this bloodline is the true "secret" behind the Templar persecution, and that they are sworn to preserve this secret bloodline.

While very little historical or scholarly data has been published on the Priory of Sion (critics have accused the group of establishing a complex hoax,) there has been a slew of mysterious deaths and kidnappings related to allegedly prominent members and Grandmasters of the Priory that beg a closer examination. If it is an elaborate hoax, why would members go to such lengths to both conceal and perpetuate its myths? Perhaps not surprisingly, the Priory's membership roster also includes a number of figures alleged to also be functioning within the structure of the dreaded Illuminati. Certainly, the wealth accumulated by the Priory is enough to make even the most casual observer view their activities with suspicion.

New Order of Templars

Formed by defrocked Cistercian monk and homosexual Jorg Lanz von Liebenfels in Austria in 1905, the Ordo Novi Templi, or New Order of Templars was a bizarre concoction of Germanic neopaganism, quack science, virulent racism, creative Biblical interpretations and supposedly divine revelations dedicated to *"further the racial self-confidence by doing pedigree and racial research, beauty contests and the founding of racist future sites in underdeveloped parts of the Earth."* To this end, Liebenfels regularly published a magazine entitled *Ostara* (named for the pre-Christian holy day of the vernal equinox), which found its strongest support among brooding pseudo-intellectuals of racist and anti-semitic circles; including a young and impressionable Adolf Hitler. In it, Liebenfels regularly upheld the superiority of the "Aryan" race, and made military and religious vows to safeguard the sanctity of the race by sterilizing and eradicating the presence of "lower" and "inferior" races.

What would seem like absurd jabberwocky of the most inane caliber by any sensible human was obviously taken quite seriously by the Third Reich. And it is safe to say that by "just following orders," the Templar concepts of sacred duty and unswerving devotion to an ideal found a tragic and convoluted conclusion in the gas chambers of Dachau and Auschwitz.

Ordo Templi Orientis

A pseudo-Masonic occult society of self-styled "Warrior Monks" sworn to uphold the religion of Thelema (an outlandish mixture of pseudo-Egyptian divine revelation supposedly received by British occultist Aleister Crowley in 1904 via a channeled text entitled *The Book of the Law*, whose central tenet can be summed up by the statement "Do what thou wilt shall be the whole of the law"), the Ordo Templi Orientis (literally "Order of the Temple of the East") seems about as far away from the Christian ideology behind the historic Knights Templar as possible. Yet its manifesto (published in 1919) maintains that in its hands is "concentrated the wisdom and knowledge" not only of several esoteric schools of thought (some entirely fictional) but also, most significantly, of the Knights Templar (of whose last Grandmaster, Jacques de Molay, was elected as "saint" in their central religious rite, the Gnostic Mass. It is also worth noting that their website indicates a physical presence in the greater Boston area called the Knights Templar Oasis.) It is also worth noting here that the same manifesto includes the Order of the Illuminati and indeed, one of their degrees is referred to as "Illuminated."

While in terms of social influence, the O.T.O. seems somewhat small (current worldwide numbers are estimated at a little more than 3,000 and most members tend to be categorized as disenchanted members of lower or middle class families), reports of drug abuse and sexual misconduct have been plaguing the cult for well over 30 years. Numerous mysterious deaths have been noted in conjunction with the O.T.O., and allegations of rape and intimidation (sometimes by higher-ups within the ranks) have been launched by former members on numerous occasions over the years.

Other Manifestations

Other recurrences of the Templar mysteries have included the Supreme Military Order of the Temple of Jerusalem (a Christian defense and charitable organization which traces its roots to the historical Knights Templar, and officially registered in France in 1919. Members have been implicated in numerous racist and anti-immigrant attacks); the Order of the Solar Temple (a secret society devoted to New Age philosophy, reincarnation, "Rosicrucian" practices and UFO contact with ties to the French far Right, many of whose members famously committed mass suicide in Switzerland in 1994 and 1995); The New Esoteric Order of the Knights Templar (a New Age and neo-Gnostic cult with ties to a noted author within the genre whose works have praised incest and whose followers have been accused of bribery and embezzlement); and the Ancient Order of Black Templars (a South American sect that practices an offbeat blend of Voodoo and Santeria, Freemasonry and neo-Gnosticism, with links to the O.T.O. and a noted Chicago cult leader known for allegations of extreme sexual misconduct and prostitution.)

Not to mention numerous groups with highly dubious claims of being the reconstituted Knights Templar, including one outfit whose membership included the Norwegian Anders Breivik, who murdered over 75 people—many of them teenagers and pre-teens—in Norway during a mass killing in 2009, citing extreme anti-Muslim and anti-immigrant motives as rationale for his attack. His manifesto, some 1500 pages of rambling and vitriolic far Right acerbity, makes numerous references to the ideals of the Templars.

Members

Since their official dissolution in 1312, the names of the original Knights Templar have been lost to history, with the exception of the more prominent members. However, members of Templar-derived ideologies and organizations are too wide to list here. Some who have been alleged to have been members have included French film maker and painter Jean Cocteau (Priory of Sion); actor John Wayne (Freemason, Order of de Molay); baseball player Babe Ruth

(Knights of Columbus); composer Claude Debussy (Priory of Sion); cartoonist Mel Blanc (Order of de Molay); musicians Daryl Hall, John Frusciante and Mick Fleetwood (Ordo Templi Orientis); actor Roy Rogers (Freemason); far Right Belgian politician Jean Francois Thiriart (Order of the Solar Temple); actor Ernest Borgnine (Freemason); Chicago mayor Richard Daley (Knights of Columbus); journalist Ed Bradley (Freemason); musician Todd Rundgren (Ordo Templi Orientis); former Secretary of State Henry Kissinger (Freemason, Illuminati); author John Steinbeck (Order of de Molay); cartoonist and innovator Walt Disney (Freemason); former Presidents Ronald Reagan and George Bush (Freemasons, Illuminati); painter and inventor Leonardo da Vinci (Priory of Sion); filmmaker Kenneth Anger (Ordo Templi Orientis); actor Jerry Orbach (Order of de Molay, Freemason); General Douglas M. MacArthur (Freemason); author Victor Hugo (Priory of Sion); singer and actor Burl Ives (Order of de Molay); photographer Robert Mapplethorpe (Ordo Templi Orientis); actor Sylvester Stallone (Freemason); composer Wolfgang Amadeus Mozart (Freemason, Illuminati); American Revolutionary Paul Revere (Freemason); Prime Minister Cecil Rhodes

(Freemason, Illuminati) and Church of Mormon founder Brigham Young (Freemason).

Chapter Three: THE ILLUMINATI

The Illuminati. The very name is enough to cause fear and revulsion in the heart of any sensible, free-thinking individual. Rumored to be the impetus behind both the American and French revolutions of the 18th century as well as both world wars, the notion of a secretive shadow organization of puppet masters pulling the strings behind every social movement—progressive or not—and every mass calamity has been the source of mass speculation and paranoia throughout history. How did an obscure Masonic offshoot established by a rogue Jesuit priest in 1776 come to encapsulate world power the likes of which is beyond the wildest dreams of even the most greedy of would-be dictators?

The truth is, as far as the Illuminati is concerned, very little bedrock evidence for their continued proliferation can be found. The ultimate nature of a secret society is just that; a secret. And perhaps no other society has been so successful in shrouding themselves in mystery, deceit and misinformation than the Order of the Illuminati. So successful that millions of Americans don't even realize they hold their trademark right in the folds of their wallet: the dollar bill. Look at the backside and observe the enigmatic eye in the pyramid, crowned by the banner "Novus Ordo Seclorum"—the New World Order. If that's not enough to convince you of the ultimate plot of their designs, then read on. What you refuse to admit just might haunt you in the end.

Origins of the Illuminati

The story of the Illuminati begins in Bavaria in 1770. A Jewish convert to Roman Catholicism, Adam Weishaupt was elected as Professor of Canon Law at the University of Ingolstadt—a chair traditionally held by a Jesuit priest. Despite a subsequent conversion to the Jesuit faith, the 22-year old Weishaupt still found himself victim of repeated rebukes and character assassination by Jesuit colleagues and superiors. Rather than retaliate, the prank-minded Weishaupt decided to form an exclusive cadre of so-called "enlightened ones" or Perfectibilists (literally, "the perfected ones") on May 1, 1776—coincidentally, the pagan holiday of Beltane—modeled after the degrees and structure of Freemasonry. The overall goal of the Illuminati was to establish a free and just society, without ecclesiastical or political tyranny in which both men and women were considered equal, and church authorities had no say. To this end, they allegedly sought freedom of speech and a complete overthrow of existing power structures, receiving funding from the House of Rothschild—both historically and currently the leading financiers in global banking—and forging alliances with Freemasonry, whose degree system they adopted into a series of ten symbolic levels: Novitiate, Minerval, Illuminated Minerval, Illuminatus Minor, Illuminatus Major, Illuminatus Drigens, Priest, Regent, Magus and Rex.

The initial six degrees appear steeped in the biblical and cabalistic mysteries of Freemasonry. Indeed, it is from these initial degrees that Weishaupt's Illuminati structure found the strongest support from existing Masonic lodges. However, at the level of Priest, the candidate was required to renounce and sever all Masonic ties, wearing an oath of devotion solely to the Illuminati. The degree of Regent extended this renunciation from conventional political and religious structures even further, with the candidate formally denouncing *all* ties to social, religious and political affiliations and was expected to extend the influence and aims of the Illuminati even further, subverting and infiltrating those very structures they denounced

(a practice reminiscent of the Hashishins covered in Chapter One.)

The order soon grew support from some of the leading political, literary and social figures of the time, including Ferdinand of Brunswick, foreign diplomat Xavier von Zwack, the writers Wolfgang von Goethe and Gottfried Herder, Duke Karl August of Saxe-Weimar, philosopher Georg Hegel, mystic Karl von Eckartshausen, the elusive Comte de Saint-Germain, and numerous Princes, Dukes and Barons from Bavaria and beyond.

Yet in 1782, delegates from a Bavarian Masonic conference—who had apparently been denied entrance to the upper echelon of the order—formally denounced the Illuminati. Pressure from both the Catholic hierarchy and Masonic lodges forced then ruler Karl Theodor to ban the Illuminati altogether, and the order was announced as dissolved in 1785. Yet there is substantial evidence that this dissolution was simply a ruse to hide the activities of the order internationally—particularly in France and the nascent America, where Illuminati tenets and doctrines had a substantial influence on both revolutions (it is known that one of the architects of the French Revolution, Jean-Joseph Mounier was a member, and there is strong evidence that Thomas Paine, John Hancock, Alexander Hamilton and Thomas Jefferson were secretly affiliated with the order.) Weishaupt himself fled to Gotha, where he was granted amnesty by Duke Ernst II and from which he continued his base of operations until his death in 1811.

As noted previously, Weishaupt drew initial support from the banking dynasty of the Rothschilds, and there is considerable evidence that members of the family took formal initiation into the lodge at its early stages. Other merchants and bankers were well known to have connections to the lodge, including the Swiss Jean Gaspard Schweizer and the Austrian Ludwig von Goldman. However, it is through the Rothschilds (whose scion, Mayer Rothschild is known to have stated, "Give me control over a nation's currency, and the law is meaningless") that Weishaupt drew his strongest financial and social support—a family dynasty that perhaps not-so-coincidentally were responsible for financing the Napoleonic wars, the establishment of the U.S. Federal Reserve in 1913 and currently own an estimated 220 banks, including the Bank of England, the Bank of Israel and the People's Bank of China, as well as controlling interests in such corporations as

Microsoft and IBM. And it is from the Rothschilds that the Illuminati perpetuates its most insidious scheme of all—a dynasty consisting of 13 distinct bloodlines.

The Illuminati in Doctrine and Practice

At this point, the reader will probably ask, "Freedom? Equality? Liberty? Isn't that the basis of our modern society? What's so insidious about freedom of speech and justice for all?" And truth be told, the ideals of freedom of opportunity and discourse ostensibly proposed by the historical Illuminati are noble and commendable. It is well worth noting that Weishaupt was a noted admirer of the philosopher Baruch Spinoza, and his fundamental text *The Ethics*. Ideally, a free market would uphold legitimate and fair trade mutually beneficial to consumers and financiers.

Given that the Rothschild dynasty currently own an estimated half of the global wealth, the notion of international free market economics in practice is simply erroneous. Given their strong prominence within similar global conglomerates of secretive elite financiers such as the Bilderberg Foundation, and their historically documented practices of financing almost every imaginable war during modern history (as well as their current and publicly stated support of Zionist causes in Israel and abroad), even the most skeptical reader should smell a rat behind the myth of free trade. Let's instead view the Rothschilds for what they are: robber barons of the most nefarious caliber imaginable. And highly successful ones at that.

The initial statutes of the Illuminati state that their goal is to *"put an end to the machinations of the purveyors of injustice, to control them without dominating them."* And while that may have been true in a progressively enlightened 18th century European framework, time has shown again and again just how quickly those ideals were corrupted by parties seeking absolute greed—and absolute power. These days, the agenda behind the Illuminati's machinations include:

1.) The establishment of a one world government, complete with one world military and police and one centralized currency. This is the true promise of the "Novus Ordo Seclorum" mentioned previously in the chapter. And both the establishment of NATO, the United

Nations and more recently, the European Union, are tangible reminders of the success of the Illuminati's mission.

2.) The establishment of a centralized bank controlling all financial transactions. At the heart of the Illuminati, greed is as critical as power and control. The existence of summits such as G-8, G-12, Bilderberg sponsored conferences, as well as the recent economic breakdowns that have plagued so much of the United States and Europe all bear the hallmarks of classic Illuminati design.

3.) Advanced micro-chip monitoring of citizens as a need for surveillance and control. This technetronic method of monitoring, as predicted by Illuminati member Zbigniew Brzezinski in his book *Between Two Ages: America's Role in the Technetronic Era*, is just one step closer to the ultimate control of the Illuminati begun with the establishment of the Social Security identification system and bar-code product identification. In time, this surveillance has also included digital monitoring of Internet activity, widespread wire tapping techniques and covert government intelligence agencies.

4.) An absolute totalitarian state in which freedom of expression is prohibited and dissenting opinion will be stifled. Widespread physical and character assassinations of those who have set out to expose Illuminati schemes has been well documented. Failing to submit to Illuminati designs, for example, the U.S. Select Service System, IRS review, and even the Registry of Motor Vehicles can and have resulted in fines and imprisonment. Other more extreme cases have included murder, blackmail, extortion, bankruptcy and arson.

It is this fourth point that is positively critical in assessing the dangers of the Illuminati. They are not merely content with a long and deliberate misinformation campaign (often disseminating conflicting information and supposed "leaks" about their operations, so that none but the most discerning observer can distinguish between falsehood and reality), but actively seek to silence dissent through physical torture and assassination. This methodology was best noted by the assassinations of both President Abraham

Lincoln and John F. Kennedy—both men whom, if not directly aware of the designs and plans of the Illuminati, certainly saw a reform in government and economic policy directly in opposition to Illuminati doctrine. Other mysterious deaths the Illuminati may be responsible include the assassination of Archduke Franz Ferdinand of Austria (which precipitated the start of World War I), the assassination of Mohandas Gandhi, the deaths of Jimmy Hoffa, Marilyn Monroe and Jayne Mansfield, the unexplained "cancer" of Bob Marley and even the recent death of erstwhile "King of Pop" Michael Jackson.

Both the internal and external symbolism of the Illuminati is rife with occult and esoteric emblems and metaphors, of which the All-seeing eye in the pyramid is perhaps the most notorious. This enigmatic device has entered the popular culture as one of the most enduring symbols, appearing everywhere from the previously noted dollar bill to popular novels, movies, comic books and video games. The ubiquity of this design has led to a public infatuation with Illuminati symbology, often unwittingly—which may indeed be part of their designs after all. In more recent times, Illuminati-based insignia has become one of the hottest trends in the music industry, with artists such as Jay-Z, Lady Gaga, Katy Perry, George Clinton, Rihanna, Madonna, Nicki Minaj and Tool—to name but a few—all openly displaying distinctively Illuminati-based symbology in videos, album covers, live shows and promotional photos, be it wittingly or unwittingly. Is this a deliberate courting of controversy? A sort of meta-ploy "wink" to the public fascination with the legend and lore of the Illuminati? Or all part of a carefully constructed plan to lure younger and more impressionable minds into faithfully adhering to Illuminati schematics?

Bloodlines of the Illuminati

As mentioned earlier, the Illuminati is headed by 13 distinct bloodlines (it is worth noting that the fascination with perpetuating bloodlines is shared in common with the previous chapter's introduction to the Priory of Sion.) Much speculation and theories of these bloodlines have been made, relating them to everything from the 12 Tribes of Israel mentioned in the book of Genesis (including the "lost" 13th tribe, commonly held to be the Khazar tribe) to the 12 signs of the Zodiac. Given that many prominent figures in government, entertainment and culture are commonly held to hold some degree of involvement with the Illuminati, it is fair to say that membership is not exclusive to these bloodlines alone. Nonetheless, the prominence of these bloodlines and their respective roles in finance and politics demands strong observance from those actively pursuing research into the Illuminati mechanism.

1.) The Rockefeller bloodline. As one of the most obvious and visible bloodlines in the Illuminati genetic strand, the Rockefeller bloodline is overseen currently by David Rockefeller, whose interests include Chase Manhattan Bank, General Electric, Mitsubishi, Exxon and Mobil Oil. The 99-year old Rockefeller also has been known to have strong ties to the CIA and the National Security Agency, and is both the founding member of the Trilateral Commission and the Council on Foreign Relations as well as serving on the Member Advisory Group of the Bilderberg Foundation. Far from denying his involvement in Illuminati schemes, Rockefeller openly admitted it in his 2002 memoirs: *"Some even believe we are part of a secret cabal working against the best interests of the United States, characterizing my family and me as internationalists and of conspiring with others around the world to build a more integrated global political and economic structure—one world, if you will. If that's the charge, I stand guilty, and I am proud of it."*

2.) The Rothschild bloodline. As previously mentioned in this chapter, the Rothschilds are one of the oldest banking families in international history, and were directly behind both the establishment of the Federal Reserve and the both the price of gold as well as its devaluation in 1971 when President Nixon ordered the cancellation of the convertibility of the U.S. dollar to gold (historically known as the "Nixon Shock.") The Rothschild bloodline is currently overseen by both Jacob Rothschild and Benjamin Rothschild, and their combined interests include the LCF Rothschild Trust, RIT Capital, Rio Tinto, a list of over 220 central banks, the Federal Reserve, and the American Bar Association.

3.) The Kennedy bloodline. A Celtic bloodline with strong ties to Freemasonry and Scottish aristocracy, and as immigration occurred towards the New World of America, organized crime and the Mafia. It is worth noting that the Kennedy bloodline, a common Gaelic surname, does not immediately implicate all Kennedys globally as Illuminati members—or even closely related. But it is stands as a testament to the ruthless blood thirst of the Illuminati that one of the most prominent descendants was assassinated for allegedly going against official Illuminati policy; the death of John F. Kennedy, which marked the end of an era in American politics and culture.

4.) The Astor bloodline. Founded by John Jakob Astor, a German-born fur trader, merchant, investor and American emigre active in the 18th and 19th centuries, the Astor family—once synonymous with the most elite of the newly monied floating in and out of America in the late 19th and early 20th centuries, particularly in New York—appears to have gone out of vogue. But their interest in politics (the British Astor bloodline has had several representatives in parliament and the Prime Ministry), finance and reputedly the international drug trade has never waned. This particular bloodline has prominent connections to British and American intelligence agencies, the Pilgrim Society, the Rhodes Scholarship Foundation and numerous private banks, real estate concerns and trusts. In addition, the Astor dynasty has had a strong relationship in Freemasonry (John Jakob Astor becoming heavily involved with New York Masonic lodges upon his immigration to the America; a strange feat for a man who supposedly spoke less than a sentence of English) and other eccentricities (one descendant, Ava Astor was an avowed occultist and believed she was the reincarnation of an Egyptian princess.)

5.) The Bundy bloodline. With strong ties to the worlds of government, research, education, science, philanthropy and Yale's secretive "Skull & Bones" society, the Bundy family isn't one of the more recognizable names to many Americans. But with Bundy family members serving in such key strategic initiatives as the CIA, atomic research (Harvey Bundy, Sr. served as the chief Pentagon liaison during the fabled "Manhattan Project" of the 1940s), the Military, some of America's leading educational institutions (such as Cornell University, Ohio State and Harvard University) and allegedly, occultism (it is known that prominent banker Harry Bundy served as a chief adept in a Masonic and Rosicrucian society in Colorado in the early 20th century), that very same lack of recognition makes them all the more dangerous.

6.) The Collins bloodline. An enigmatic bloodline with strong ties to military intelligence, law, literature, education and, strangely enough, the church. The latter becomes all the more astonishing when it is revealed that some of the more prominent figures in the bloodline have been actively involved in Freemasonry, Rosicrucianism and the occult. Numerous family members have been implicated in sex trafficking and organized crime over the years; leading one to watch clearly both the above-ground activities as well as the more clandestine, shadowy natures of this bloodline.

7.) The DuPont bloodline. Best known as heirs to the vast chemical and pharmaceutical dynasty established in 1802 as a gunpowder mill by French emigre E.I. du Pont, this bloodline also maintains strong connections to the American government, with numerous paid representatives serving in key positions in the House of Representatives, Congress and local politics in the state of Delaware. With an estimated combined wealth well into hundreds of billions of dollars and strong ties to both the Astor and Rockefeller bloodlines, the family played a critical role in securing negotiations for the Louisiana Purchase in 1803, which helped expand the territory of the Americas westward. More recently, the DuPont family made headlines in 1997, when heir John DuPont—an active philanthropist and sports enthusiast who had been diagnosed as paranoid and psychopathic—was convicted of the murder of Olympic wrestler Dave Schultz. However, the family's connection with several other mysterious deaths and disappearances indicate this may not have been likely to be the first instance of foul play; nor is it likely to be the last.

8.) The Freeman bloodline. Here, the link to the previous chapter's Priory of Sion is made implicit, as one of the more recent and imminent members of the Priory was one Gaylord Freeman, who served as Grandmaster from 1963 until 1981 (although, in keeping with the Priory's innate vows of secrecy, the elderly Freeman publicly denied any involvement or even knowledge of the existence of the society.) A well-respected financier, Freeman served as Chairman of the First National Bank of Chicago, and was a known advisor to both the Nixon and Ford administrations, also serving on the board of the Rockefeller-founded Trilateral Commission. In addition, members of the Freeman family have known connections with numerous philanthropies as well as serving on the board of the Anti-Defamation League of B'nai B'rith.

9.) The Li bloodline. An extremely elusive bloodline, operating out of Asia and the South Pacific. It is estimated that members of the Li bloodline include financiers, investors and even presidents and premiers in Hong Kong, Singapore, and The People's Republic of China (it has been well documented that David Rockefeller had extensive relations with Chinese premier Li Peng in the 1980s.) The Li bloodline also has extensive ties to the Tongs and other Triads of Chinese organized crime. Above-ground, this bloodline maintains interests in Canadian Imperial, Cavendish International, Bank of Commerce, Hong Kong Electric, and American Express, as well as maintaining international relations in trading and financing with the U.S.

10.) The Onassis bloodline. In a DNA strand already consisting of family dynasties who have entered the public lexicon as being synonymous with untold wealth, the Onassis bloodline may be among the more famous. Shipping magnate Aristotle Onassis gained notoriety as the husband of the widowed Jacqueline Kennedy in 1968, while his brother and archrival Stavros Niarchos maintained an equally impressive shipping empire, and was rumored to be one of the instigators behind the Suez Crisis of 1956 (a crisis that sought removal of then-Egyptian President Nasser and effectively crippled transportation along the Suez Canal.) The Onassis bloodline has been rumored to have involvement with extortion and bribery tactics since at least WW II (working in collusion with the U.S. and Greek governments) and has been implicated in numerous mysterious kidnappings and deaths (often mysterious drug "overdoses")—including that of Princess Grace of Monaco. Upon the elder Onassis' death in 1975, Niarchros took control of the bloodline until his death in 1996. It is not certain who currently oversees the dynasty, but there are some indicators that it may be Niarchos' son Spyros, who currently maintains close friendships with numerous financiers and premiers across Europe and the Middle East.

11.) The Reynolds bloodline. Best known as the progenitors of both R.J. Reynolds & Co. as well as Reynolds Metals, the bloodline maintains an estimated wealth of approximately $80 Billion dollars in addition to their monopolization of industries including agriculture and manufacturing. Known for funding lobbyists and research, the Reynolds bloodline has worked closely in conjunction with several U.S. Senators and Congressmen over the course of some 80 years, orchestrating bribes and payoffs and allegedly working in close conjunction with both organized crime and transportation unions.

12.)   The Russell bloodline. With its unique blend of biblical prophecy and apocalyptic rapture, the Jehovah's Witnesses sect of evangelical Christianity—which maintains over 9 million adherents worldwide—seems like an unlikely source to find an Illuminati bloodline. Yet its founder, Charles Taze Russell, not only introduced his own eschatological fervor into the Illuminati gene pool, but his ideological descendants—numbering some 120,000 congregations—have been alleged to spread chief Illuminati doctrines, with successful civil rights legislations in several countries; as well as high-profile investigations into criminal and sexual abuse reports on behalf of their congregations. What makes it all the more remarkable is that Russell shares the same blood relation to prominent Freemasons and other shadowy organizations; including Yale's Skull & Bones fraternity, of whom it is said it is funded and operated by the legal trust of the Russell corporation. It is worth noting that the late Michael Jackson was raised as a Jehovah's Witness until his disassociation in 1987. He is reported to have had a long-standing interest in the Illuminati, and his death in 2009 is still under serious scrutiny—not least of all from family members, who still maintain adherence with the sect.

13.)   The Van Duyn bloodline. One of the more obscure bloodlines that make up the Illuminati. It is said that they are descendants from early Dutch settlers of Manhattan in the 17th century, and amassed a fortune as traders, merchants and manufacturers. It is, however, known that one of the founding members of the Planned Parenthood Federation of America (which, in addition to providing affordable medical counseling also provides and encourages birth control and abortion) was one Edward Van Duyn, an American physician active in the 1920s and 1930s. Planned Parenthood is known to have received funding from trusts and foundations associated or bearing the direct name of the Astor, Rockefeller and Reynolds bloodlines. Another interesting Van Duyn connection maybe the radical Dutch agitator and anarchist Roel Van Dujin, who as public founder of the Provos party, orchestrated numerous riots and disturbances throughout the Netherlands in the 1960s and 1970s.

Other prominent families who have been known to intermarry into these bloodlines have included the Ford family; the Vanderbilt family; the Hearst family; the Carnegie family; and the Dodge family.

Members

One of the ultimate goals of any secret society, as stated previously, is the perpetuation of secrets. And as the penultimate covert secret society, the Illuminati have nearly 250 years and countless wealth behind them enabling them to specialize in psychological operations and misinformation tactics of the most advanced sort. Perhaps it's all the more fitting that the very term 'Illuminati' translates to the 'Enlightened ones'; in Latin, the name *Lucifer* comes from the words *lux ferro*, or "bearer of light."

Outside of the above-mentioned bloodlines, there is no accurate count of Illuminati membership. There are no official records of meetings, no official membership rosters and no record of precedings. They are indeed, the archetypal secret society.

Yet over the years, numerous names have been brought up in conjunction with the Illuminati; names which, upon close examination reveal common threads that defy mere coincidence and take on a decidedly more sinister hue:

American pediatrician and physician Dr. Benjamin Spock; director Steven Spielberg; music mogul Rick Rubin; actor Tom Cruise; British monarch Queen Elizabeth II; billionaire investor Warren Buffett; Secretary of State Hillary Clinton; musician Paul McCartney; Lee Harvey Oswald assassin Jack Ruby; British Prime Minister Winston Churchill; former Eisenhower Secretary of State John Foster

Dulles; actress Angelina Jolie; talk show pioneer Johnny Carson; economist John Maynard Keynes; media mogul Oprah Winfrey; former presidents George H.W. Bush, Sr. and George W. Bush, Jr.; children's programming pioneer Jim Henson; British Prime Minister Benjamin Disraeli; technology innovators Steve Jobs and Bill Gates; musician David Bowie; Israeli president Benjamin Netanyahu; entertainer Bob Hope; Former Soviet President Mikhail Gorbachev; billionaire Richard Branson; artist Salvador Dali; former vice presidents Dick Cheney and Gerald Ford; former presidents Richard Nixon and Franklin D. Roosevelt; musician Prince; diplomat Henry Kissinger; actor Nicolas Cage; former Prime Minister Tony Blair; political pundit William F. Buckley, Jr.; hip-hop producer Dr. Dre; Federal Reserve chairmen Alan Greenspan and Ben Bernanke; basketball player Dennis Rodman; actress and diplomat Shirley Temple Black; Former presidents Dwight D. Eisenhower, Herbert Hoover and Ronald Reagan; director George Lucas; U.N. founder Alger Hiss; and television evangelist Pat Robertson.

Chapter Four: FREEMASONRY

Next to the Illuminati (of whom they are closely associated with) no other society has spawned more rumors and allegations than the Freemasons. Ostensibly a fraternal organization devoted to charitable deeds, civic obligation, brotherhood and the betterment of the individual, Freemasonry has wielded a considerable amount of power over political, economic and social spheres over the past three hundred years. How then did this strange amalgamation of disparate men, rooted in obscure ritual, pageantry and secrecy, come to be known and reviled as the architects behind numerous revolutions, wars and social changes?

The institution of Freemasonry describes itself as *"a beautiful system of morality, veiled in allegory and illustrated by symbols."* Such a description is both highly suggestive and while open to interpretation, seems to pose no immediate threat to the general population other than a collection of bizarre symbolism masked by a frequently transparent veil of secrecy (both the rituals and doctrines of Freemasonry have been openly published, and accessible to even non-affiliated parties.) In fact, in comparison to the vogue in which Freemasonry swept throughout

Europe and America from its early foundings up until the first half of the 20th Century, Freemasonry—which today only numbers approximately 1.2 million members in the U.S. (a far cry from their heyday of the 1960s where membership reached close to 5 million) with numbers predicted to drop considerably in the next twenty years—seems an almost archaic and outdated throwback to a period of elaborately costumed galas and mens' only meetings. Hardly worth serious time or consideration.

Yet, as the last chapter has shown, there has been considerable parallels and a mutually beneficial historical relationship between Freemasonry and the Illuminati. Virtually all of the founding fathers of the United States were indeed Freemasons, as has been ably documented elsewhere; In fact virtually *all* presidencies have either been manned by Masons or included key cabinet members who were affiliated *until* the presidency of Abraham Lincoln (whose assassination is still subject for much speculation.) And the influence of the Illuminati bears a striking resemblance to the U.S. Constitution and Bill of Rights. Coincidence? Or is the institution of Freemasonry a training ground of sorts for Illuminati candidacy?

As I mentioned in the introduction, unlike the clandestine nature of the Illuminati, Freemasonry may be the classic *overt* secret society. Membership is open to all males, 18 years of age, joining of their own free will and professing a belief not only in a Supreme Being (and that definition is *very* loosely defined) but a belief in the betterment of the individual and society. All that is needed is the sponsorship and recommendation of at least two members of a Masonic lodge.

With a highly visible advertising and PR campaign in recent years (some of which knowingly nods at their "mysterious" and conspiratorial reputation) in a last-ditch effort to find new candidates from younger generations— most of whom probably find the structure and rite of the institution hopelessly dull and corny— Freemasonry is hardly the elusive and elite society whispered about in conjunction with the magnates and leaders of bygone days. If anything, it may be compared to a shell of its former influence and glory. Yet sometimes shells can hide some very strange ghosts, indeed.

Like barnacles attached to the hull of a boat, Freemasonry and the Illuminati may be inextricably linked. How this influence came to be, is another story altogether...

The Origins of Freemasonry

The origins of Freemasonry, as Masonic apologists and authors are so fond of repeating, are forever lost to the sands of time; thereby grafting a highly dubious insinuation of ancient legacy upon the history of Masonic Craft. How and why these mysterious legacies of ancient pedigree are so integral to Freemasonry may be largely a result of an unconscious need to equate longevity with relevance (a notion discarded with the sudden rise of success of institutions such as McDonald's or science fiction movies in the immediate years following WWII.)

Whatever the case may be, the first organized Masonic activity is generally held to be founded on June 24, 1717 with the assembly of the first United Grand Lodge of England. Prior to this, there were loosely organized guilds of what has come to be known as "Speculative Masonry"; that is, loose affiliates of like-minded individuals forming a mutual aid society modeled after the stonemason guilds of the 13th and 14th centuries, in whom they found an ideal allegory for non-denominational religious beliefs and the interpretation of biblical parables as metaphors for both the "universal brotherhood of man" (an idea none too popular in still pre-Enlightenment times) and historic allusions. Some of these guilds have been proven to be in existence as early as the 16th century (during which time the stonemason guilds had been officially abolished by Archbishop Thomas Cranmer, leader of the English Reformation, in 1548), but it wasn't until at least 150 years later that these guilds met to form a unified front.

Over the next 70 years, Freemasonry began to grow considerably among all walks of life throughout Europe, petitioning as it did a relatively egalitarian ethos of brotherhood, justice and labor. As the popularity of Freemasonry grew, so did the need to formalize established constitutions, dictates and most famously, their degree structure and rituals. Space permits us from delving at all into the structure of these ritual or degrees, other than to state that they are rooted in biblical, classical and cabalistic symbolism and historical allegory (including the introduction of the myth of the Knights Templar as introduced in Chapter Two), the meaning of which is revealed through successive degrees.

As the popularity of Freemasonry migrated throughout both Europe and the New World, many of the leading ideologues of the time became enamored of its tenets, which held that the equality of all men was indeed a demonstrable fact (a parallel with the Hermetic axiom of "As above, so below" alluded to in this book's introduction.) Frenchmen such as Jean-Jacques Rousseau, Voltaire and Montesquieu—all leading figures of the Enlightenment whose philosophies would have an inestimable influence on the formation of the American Constitution—were confirmed Freemasons, as were American founding fathers such as Benjamin Franklin, Thomas Jefferson and George Washington.

In order to place the popularity of such secretive organizations in context, we should take into account that such movements served a two-fold purpose: the first is to provide a relative harbor where such ideals could be championed and discussed openly without fear of reprisal from reigning political ideologies who saw egalitarianism as inimical to their very structure. The second is that of a social mechanism. Much like today, even intellectuals needed a place free of judgment where they could relax and enjoy the fellowship and camaraderie of like-minded individuals. One drastic, if relevant, example would be the infamous Hellfire Club of Sir Francis Dashwood (of which Benjamin Franklin was known to be a member of)—a libertine society in the 18th century, consisting of both British aristocrats and commoners alike that was said to harbor secret services of devil worship; although in all likelihood, this was just a colorful and poetic metaphor for perpetual drunkenness, as opposed to legitimate Satanic practices.

As both the ideals and the popularity of Freemasonry continued to filter throughout both continents, so did its interaction with both increasingly progressive thought as well as existing Hermetic and Rosicrucian organizations—both of which shared common philosophical backgrounds. The need for a more inclusive attitude as well as allowance for diversity of opinion and ritual faced the various Grand Lodges throughout Europe and the Americas. Their decision was to establish a strict guideline of observance, practices and ritual lore in which those outside of its pale—such as lodges which chose to allow female participation—bore the stigma of being known as Irregular, or Illicit Masonry. Some customs, such as those of Prince Hall Masonry (which developed among freed slaves in the late 18th and early 19th centuries) were permitted as separate but recognized Masonic entities by Grand Lodge edicts. However, those who continued to operate—at times clandestinely—as Illicit Masonic observances were the subject of outright hostility and vilification. And it is to these illicit chapters that we must observe if we wish to see the shadow side of Masonry in action.

Freemasonry in Practice

In Freemasonry, freedom represented liberty and equality in all sectors of life, inasmuch as it demanded the worship of a Supreme Being (whom Masons to this day refer to as the Great Architect of the Universe) whose dictates the Free and Accepted Mason swore to uphold and present himself according to (it is interesting to note that the Freemasons might be considered early pioneers of interfaith practices currently in fashion.) The Masonic candidate was considered to be a seeker after light (see the last chapter to note the parallels between Freemasonry and the Illuminati); and having found it metaphorically in the institution of Freemasonry, was expected to act as a similar beacon both those in his community as well as his fellow Masonic brethren.

But for the Illicit or Irregular Mason, this freedom represented liberty from an altogether different sort; freedom from conventional religious structures, as well as freedom from the burdens of moral dictates they enabled (again, eerily similar to the teachings established some seven hundred years earlier by Hassan i Sabbah and the Order of Hashishins.) A pertinent example was how the movement spread into Russia in the mid 19th century. Both imperial Russia, its nobility and even its gentry at the time were plagued by violent attacks from radical anarchist and nihilist entities (of which, no better loosely fictionalized example could be given than in Dostoyevsky's classic novel "The Possessed")—many of whom forged alliances and cells in the Masonic lodges, both regular and irregular, sweeping across Russia at the time. It is well known that the leading anarchist theorist Mikhail Bakunin (who once wrote that the revolutionary must seek *"the unchaining of what is today called the evil passions and the destruction of what is called public order. Let us put our trust in the eternal spirit which destroys and annihilates only because it is the unsearchable and eternally creative source of all life - the passion for destruction is wholly a creative passion"*) was a member of one such lodge, and also called for the abolition of marriage, property and the complete reversal of all social and religious institution; a charge most commonly associated with the Illuminati.

It is also well known that Bakunin enjoyed frequent meetings with *Communist Manifesto* author Karl Marx and was a direct influence on February revolution of 1848 and the Paris Commune uprising of 1871, both of which sought to replace the French republic with a more avowedly socialist design. Could it be that the spectres of communism and socialism that haunted much of the 20th century has its root in Masonic ideals?

In America, however, the noble ideals of equality and freedom supposedly germane to Freemasonry found its diametrical opposite in the Civil War and its twisted offspring, the Ku Klux Klan. Albert Pike, a Boston born turned officer in the Confederate army, was a top-ranking 33rd degree Freemason (the highest of degrees Regular and Accepted Freemasonry recognizes) and author of the esteemed work *Morals and Dogma of Freemasonry* (a work which is replete with extensive references lauding the figure of Lucifer; again, redolent of an uncanny parallel to the Illuminati.)

Pike, who would early on in his career pen hymns to unnamed pagan gods, also had a role in establishing the Ku Klux Klan, along with Nathaniel Bedford Forrest (himself a fellow Freemason)—a secret society itself which swore to uphold the rights of white citizenry and landowners from what they viewed as the threat from newly freed slaves. This society, replete with elaborate code words, costumes, and dreadful oaths of secrecy went on to initiate some of the most appalling and cowardly acts of widespread violence and murder, acts which they happily admit to continuing to this very day. Numerous other top ranking confederate soldiers also took part in the establishment of the Klan, including, including Gen. William Henry Wallace, Col. Henry Alexander Wise and even (so it is rumored) General Robert E. Lee. Which gives pause to wonder how sincere was Freemasonry's supposed avowal of freedom, equality and liberty if some of its chief proponents were unabashed supporters of the most senselessly barbaric and dehumanizing institutions in American history?

Perhaps more interestingly and tellingly were a series of letters Pike wrote in 1871 to a leading Masonic diplomat and politician named Giuseppe Mazzini, the organizer of an Italian political party named *La giovine Italia*, which was devoted to the unification of the separate states and kingdoms across the Italian peninsula (and whose slogan was "One, Independent, Free Republic.") In them, Pike predicts the coming of three separate world wars which was necessary to sow and ferment interior conflicts, leading up to one great and inevitable social cataclysm; a trial by fire after which the doctrine of pure light and reason would reign (again, signifying roots in Illuminati doctrine.)

Masonry had already been well established in Italy by the year 1877 and the formation of the Lodge *Propaganda Massonica* in Turin. After WW II, Freemasonry was all but dormant in Italy due to both the banning of Masonry by Mussolini's regime as well as the scrutiny of the Christian Democrat party then in power (it is interesting to see how strong a hold Freemasonry took in Italy, given the notorious animosity between Masons and the Catholic Church.)

However, a renegade but recognized Freemason by the name of Licio Gelli (known himself to show pro-Fascist and Nazi sympathies) reconstituted the moribund Lodge as Propaganda Due, or P-2 in the late 1960s, outside the jurisdiction of the Grand Lodge of Italy. Within a matter of a few short years, Gelli was known to have influence over the highest echelons of Italian society, including the sovereign state of the Vatican—with whom, it has been shown, Gelli allied himself with the business of helping to harbor Nazi war criminals in hiding.

In fact, Gelli's influence was so widespread that P-2's influence began to be seen as a shadowy, secret government, virulently opposed against the Italian Communist Party (of whose members the Lodge committed several notable kidnappings and subsequent murders) and regularly supported by the governments of Brazil, Nicaragua, Uruguay and Argentina (of whose dictator, Juan Peron, Gelli repeatedly referred to as being his close, personal friend.) When Gelli's personal list of P-2 members was discovered in 1981 following the Vatican banking scandal (in which the Vatican was accused of being the main shareholder of Banco Ambrisiano, a private bank that also operated as a money laundering source for various members of the Mafia—a scandal which left bank president and P-2 member Roberto Calvi dead in a likely P-2 assassination), its roster numbered forty-three members of the Italian parliament, three cabinet ministers, the head and sub-heads of every major branch of the Italian military, Italy's top financiers and bankers, major media figures and even future Prime Minister Silvio Berlusconi (of whom Gelli stated in 2003 in reference to, "All is becoming a reality little by little, piece by piece. To be truthful, I should have had the copyright to it. Justice, TV, public order. I wrote [Berlusconi's administration] thirty years ago.")

Also figuring prominently on Gelli's list were noted members of the Gambino and Lucchese mafia syndicates. Yet despite several—possibly hundreds of—unexplained deaths and disappearances, bribery and corruption charges, and known involvement with military takeovers in South America, the 95 year old Gelli not only remains a free man to this day, but was nominated for a Noble Prize in literature in 1996 by none other than Mother Teresa of Calcutta. Perhaps not all that surprising at all; rumors of Gelli's involvement with NATO and CIA-sponsored campaigns of sowing anti-communist sentiment abroad have been heard for decades.

Italy wasn't the sole totalitarian regime to outlaw Freemasonry; secret societies of all sorts had been banned with the rise of Hitler and the Nazi Party in 1933. Yet the influence of

Freemasonry in the German political spectrum had been felt for decades prior, most notably during the reign of Prussian Chancellor Otto von Bismarck. Bismarck, a 33rd-degree Mason, helped annex and unify the outlying states of the German confederation, paving the way for the second Reich Wilhelm I of Prussia (himself allegedly a 33rd-degree Mason) during a series of bloody wars (including the Franco-Prussian War), eventually becoming the first elected Chancellor of Germany. Ironically, it was Wilhelm I's grandson, Wilhelm II's reign that helped usher in WWI—itself, frequently implicated as being evidence of an Illuminati plot. It is known now that von Bismarck was granted the establishment of a Supreme German Council of Freemasonry by none other than Albert Pike; a fact that, in light of Pike's prophecies to Giuseppe Mazzini, makes the previous sentence all the more damning.

Even the Ordo Templi Orientis, discussed in Chapter Two, was established in 1895 in Germany as a "Academica Masonica" by the Austrian chemist Karl Kellner and Dr. Theodor Reuss—a singer, journalist, police informant, spy and one time lover of Karl Marx's daughter, Eleanor. It is known that Reuss made connections in Munich in 1880 with descendants of Weishaupt's original Bavarian Illuminati, and received a charter to revive it. Indeed, one of the Order's initial manifesto purports to teach *"the key to all the secrets of Freemasonry"* as well as those of *"sexual magic"*; and since numerous allegations of rape (the O.T.O is one of few Masonically-derived bodies to allow an equal female presence), assault and coercion—to speak nothing of mysterious deaths and known drug use—one wonders how to interpret those secrets.

Chinese Freemasonry is officially banned by the People's Republic of China, although a Grand Lodge was formed in Taiwan in 1949 that is officially recognized by the United Grand Lodge of England. However, there are parallel roots in the emergence of mutual aid societies developing along mainland China in the 16th and 17th centuries, and it is quite probable that Freemasonry could have been established via trade routes in the country as early as the late 1700s. Regardless, the intermingling of Freemasonry with the new Chinese immigrant culture in the U.S. began in the early 19th century with the rise of the East-West maritime trade and the construction of the transcontinental railroad, and by the 1870s there were Chinese Masonic lodges meeting in various major metropolitan cities throughout the U.S.

However with the necessary emergence of the notorious Triads of Chinese-American legend (themselves initially mutual aid societies devoted to aid Asian families either threatened by xenophobic sentiments or to assist in helping them settle abroad) during approximately the same time, by the 1940s the migration of Chinese, Taiwanese and Hong Kong natives took on a decidedly more criminally-minded hue than merely the colorful customs of fraternal associations. Chinese Masonic lodges have known to harbor high-level drug dealers and provide a blanket covering for extortion, gambling, prostitution and counterfeiting activities, all safely camouflaged by the already secretive Masonic square and compass. There's no way of knowing how deep the extent of criminal syndicate infiltration with Masonic lodges is just yet, but according to police and FBI reports it has been occurring widely since the 1970s—at the very least.

Dangers of Freemasonry

As stated in the introduction, there's little reason to assume that all Freemasons are behind a single unified plan for global domination. In fact, few Masons even make it to the higher echelon—most are content on enjoying a night out without their wives, dressed in outlandish costumes, referring to one another by exalted names and secret handshakes. A grown up version of a tree-house club.

Would these grown-up boys be so quick to knowingly address one another with a wink and a nod if they knew the true history and shadowy elements behind Freemasonry?

I chose to omit some of the more outlandish accusations leveled against Freemasonry in this chapter and instead chose to rely on verifiable facts. Not because there may not be justifiable basis in those accusations, but because the dedicated researcher would have an easier time trying to discern what goes on behind those closed doors if presented with concrete reality instead of opinionated fancy. The real danger in Freemasonry is not necessarily that of unmitigated evil lurking behind the *sanctum sanctorum* of your local Masonic lodge. No, the true danger is how quickly seemingly noble virtues can be denigrated to the spheres of greed, crime, bigotry, murder and the corruption provided by unassailable power. And how quickly those virtues can be integrated into a schematic of control and domination on a global political and social scale. Unless, of course, those noble virtues were simply part of that schematic all along...

Members

In addition to the previously mentioned parties in this chapter, known current and historical Freemasons have included: Emperor of Mexico Agustin I; astronaut Edward "Buzz" Aldrin; French emperor Napoleon Bonaparte I; author Mark Twain; automotive pioneer Walter Chrysler; aviator Charles Lindbergh; poet Alexander Pope; actor Richard Pryor; Supreme Court Chief Justice Earl Warren; silent film director Louis B. Mayer; FBI Director J. Edgar Hoover; Turkish leader Mustafa Kemal Ataturk; escape artist Harry Houdini; Bolivian leader Simon Bolivar; silent film director Cecil B. DeMille; former Russian Czar Alexander I; former Presidents James Garfield, William McKinley and James Monroe; boxer Sugar Ray Robinson; King of Sweden and Norway Charles XIII; artist Marc Chagall; composer Felix Mendelssohn; British King William IV; author Arthur Conan Doyle; Bell Aircraft founder Lawrence Dale Bell; automobile pioneer Henry Ford; Former Presidents James K. Polk, Andrew Jackson and Calvin Coolidge; boxing promoter

Don King; Apple co-founder Steve Wozniak; Chief Justice Earl Warren; Mt. Rushmore sculptors and designers Gutzon and Lincoln Borglum; explorer Richard Francis Burton; former presidents Harry S. Truman and Theodore Roosevelt; American frontiersman Davy Crockett; Belgian King Leopold I; politician Bob Dole; philosopher Friedrich Schiller; Church of Mormon co-founder Joseph Smith; Revolutionary War general Benedict Arnold; Supreme Court Justice Thurgood Marshall; British King Edward VIII; philosopher Johann Gottlieb Fichte; explorer Hiram Bingham; and former presidents Warren G. Harding and Lyndon B. Johnson.

Chapter Five: THE TRILATERAL COMMISSION AND THE BILDERBERG GROUP

In the altogether elusive lore of secret societies, no two entities seem more unlikely of inclusion than the Trilateral Commission and the Bilderberg Group. Both are well-documented, if private, institutions whose existence as advisors on topics of global political and economic affairs have been well documented. Neither claim any illustrious (if dubious) heritage or claims to hidden "wisdom" or any esoteric underpinnings that have marked so many of the groups that we have covered to date. In fact, both seem like standard geopolitical think-tanks, with all the trappings of banality, bureaucracy and docile harmlessness that one would expect from any supposedly "non-partisan" socioeconomic institution. Minutes and synopses from regular conferences are routinely updated on their website, and both foundations appear to operate with the relative transparency belying any supposed clandestine activity.

First impressions aren't always correct.

The truth is, behind their veil of seeming mundanity and discourse of fostering "growing interdependence," there is a definitive ethos of globalization that appears at times downright identical to historical Illuminati doctrine and methodology. So identical, that the mutually recurring names and cross-pollination between all three entities are hardly coincidental. And with key advisors on both entities including top financiers, government "advisors" and subsequent appointed economists, the end net worth between the two just *could* ostensibly foster leading breakthroughs in scientific research and development, end poverty or world hunger, or ensure an adequate global infrastructure of resources for developing communities worldwide. Or it could be one more step towards a centralized world government skeptics have been laughing at threats of all these years.

Synarchy and its Malcontents

The purpose of this book is to provide a historical overview of secret societies and the threat they pose to the global population. It is not meant to purport any political overview, serve as an economic primer or foster xenophobic sentiment. The educated reader can, and likely will, come across suitable works in which he can make an informed viewpoint in this regard; and in all likelihood, he or she has already done so. But in researching this book, one particular strand tends to serve as a unifying factor behind the seeming disparity of these groups. That factor is that of a singular philosophy that seeks to construct a homogenized culture and governmental structure, wielding an inordinate and unassailable power, aided by the twin guardians of finance and cronyism. One in which dissent is silenced—by acts of violence if need be—by force, and control exerted over every aspect of its citizens lives, often unknowingly.

In order to understand how the theory of such a global totalitarian regime could possibly manifest, we need to go back to its roots—ones which date back to the 19th century and which lay in an obscure political doctrine entitled synarchy. And one which was first proposed by a French occultist and known Freemason named Joseph Alexandre Saint-Yves d'Alveydre.

As mentioned in the previous chapter, the emergence of radical anarchist, socialist and nihilist philosophies had entered into vogue in Europe during the latter half of the 19th century, inspired by writers such as Bakunin, Marx, P.J. Proudhon, and Karl Heinzen (who wrote that *"the principal agent of historical progress is murder.")*   Simultaneously, there was a resurgence in Hermetic and Rosicrucian philosophies throughout the artistic beau-monde at the time, with even noted philosophers in support of rationalism and reason becoming entranced with the mystical doctrines. Central to this doctrine was the notion of an elite and unseen cabal of "secret chiefs" that guided the progress and evolution of man's spiritual and even material progress (a trait that should now be evident as common to Freemasonry and the doctrine of the Illuminati.)

Also in vogue was the notion of Hegelian dialectics, which held that the principles of thesis, antithesis and synthesis were the rational successive conclusions behind all phenomena but also that this model could apply to large scale political constructs as opposed to the merely subjective queries of ontology. One of the early adopters of this strange graft of dialectical logic with esoteric philosophy was the aforementioned D'Alveydre, whose solution to the threat of nihilistic social breakdown was to counter it with what he termed *synarchy*, or *synarchism*, which translates to "joint rule."

In his work *La France vraie* (*The Real France*), D'Alveydre put forth that the concept of synarchy—his idealized form of government derived from bizarre beliefs about Ancient Egypt and Atlantis being harmonious societies existing as an organic "unity"—rested on two pillars. The first being that synarchy represented a 'Government by an enlightened elite.' Naturally, the "elite" themselves would decide on the definition of "enlightenment"; presumably it referred to those who were in agreement with them. The second would be the polar opposite of anarchy, where if a minimal necessary state was needed it would have minimal control, in synarchy the state would have maximal control over each aspect of individual's lives. To this end, D'Alveydre and his followers predicted the rise of a Federal European Union, creating a classless but hierarchal mega-state, run by an enlightened elite with neither conservative nor liberal policies but ones whose enlightenment entitled them to decide and control every single aspect of the lives of the populace.

Despite the legitimate threats of both World Wars effectively ending the luxury provided to the leisure class to pursue this crackpot mystical political theory, its fundamental ideas began to seep throughout Europe. Both Fascism and the Communism of the USSR are essentially elaborations on fundamental synarchic principles, and during the second World War, French Synarchists collaborated with German occupying forces in Vichy France on grounds of preserving the model of state apparatus. Of course, the world has learned from the mistakes of totalitarian regimes, and would never seek absolute control over an absolute populace in the 70 or so years since?

Unless, that is, you ask residents of the European Union. Who can count a predominantly high number of representatives among the most visible advisors of both the Trilateral Commission and the Bilderberg Group.

The Trilateral Commission

Formed in 1973 by David Rockefeller (whom you will no doubt remember from Chapter 3), The Trilateral Commission bills itself as a private commission formed of *"citizens of Japan, Europe and North America to foster closer cooperation among these core industrialized areas of the world with shared leadership responsibilities in the wider international system."* From its founding declaration:

"Growing interdependence is a fact of life of the contemporary world. It transcends and

influences national systems... To be effective in meeting common problems, Japan, Western Europe, and North America will have to consult and cooperate more closely, on the basis of equality, to develop and carry out coordinated policies on matters affecting their common interests... refrain from unilateral actions incompatible with their interdependence and from actions detrimental to other regions... [and] take advantage of existing international and regional organizations and further enhance their role. The Commission hopes to play a creative role as a channel of free exchange of opinions with other countries and regions. Further progress of the developing countries and greater improvement of East-West relations will be a major concern."

Yet critics have been quick to point out that this "fostering of interdependence" has done little to ameliorate fundamental disparities of exchange, but has exacerbated existing crises of common interest; in certain cases manipulating them to suit their own agendas. One early critic was former Senator Barry Goldwater, who suggested it was a *"coordinated attempt to seize control and consolidate the four centers of power: political, monetary, intellectual and ecclesiastical in the creation of an economic* world power superior to the political governments of the nation-states involved." While from the opposite end of the political spectrum, leading Leftist semiotician Noam Chomsky implies that the Commission is *"concerned with trying to induce what they call 'more moderation in democracy'; turning people back to passivity and obedience so they don't put so many constraints on state power."*

Yet it was up to the aforementioned Rockefeller—along with Trilateral co-founder Zbigniew Brzezinski—to effectively select and choose the several hundred leading minds of finance and industry to serve on the initial committee; essentially ensuring that the global financial interests of the Rockefeller empire would be best served by its committee members. And it was largely their joint ploy that helped elect then-Georgia Governor Jimmy Carter the presidential seat in 1976. And given the Rockefeller's vested personal portfolio of real estate investments in Atlanta was estimated to be in the $5 Billion range during the 1970s alone, is it any wonder that Atlanta was known as the "Rockefeller Center of the South?"

Yet money alone isn't sufficient to sway the minds of a general populace. The collective human experience shows us that there must be a concrete series of organizing principles and guidelines—no matter how absurd or irrational—in order to develop (or perhaps more appropriately, *suggest*) the approval or disapproval of a mass population. So before you read the following words of Trilateral Commission co-founder and former National Security Advisor for President Carter Zbigniew Brzezinski (from his 1970 opus *Between Two Ages,*) you may want to keep an open mind about the previous section's description of synarchy:

"In the absence of social consensus society's emotional and rational needs may be fused -- mass media makes this easier to achieve -- in the person of an individual who is seen as...making the necessary innovations in the social order.

"Such a society would be dominated by an elite whose claim to political power would rest on allegedly superior scientific know-how. Unhindered by the restraints of traditional liberal values, this elite would not hesitate to achieve its political ends by the latest modern techniques for influencing public behavior and

keeping society under close surveillance and control.

"Though Stalinism may have been a needless tragedy for both the Russian people and communism as an ideal, there is the intellectually tantalizing possibility that for the world at large it was, as we shall see, a blessing in disguise."

Which can be compared with the statements of Rockefeller himself after his 1973 visit to the People's Republic of China:

"The social experiment of China under Chairman Mao's leadership is one of the most important and successful in human history." (New York Times, "From a China Traveler," August 10, 1973) *"... the family unit is broken up...The children are taken away from the parents and placed in government-run nurseries...The parents may see their children once a week and when they see them they cannot show affection toward the children. The idea is to have the children and the family sever their affection and direct it toward the state. Names are taken away from the children and they are given numbers. There is no individual identity... The commune system is destroying*

morality in Red China: There is no morality because the love of the family is taken away. There is no honesty and respect among men or between men. There is no human dignity: they are all like animals. There is no guilt associated with murder of individuals for the improvement of the state..."

Both of which may shed an entirely new light on the proposition of "fostering interdependence between nations."

The Bilderberg Group

Within the realm of overt secret societies, the Bilderberg Group enjoys a certain notoriety as operating under policies of exclusivity and privacy. Paradoxically, it has never denied its existence, and lists annual members and chairmen of its conferences openly, even publishing its findings and reports. Yet surrounding them remains a veil of secrecy and elitism that causes the casual observer to ponder what the real motivations are behind their seemingly diplomatic and benevolent facade.

The Bilderberg conferences were established in 1954 as a private three-day conference between approximately 60 leaders of politics, finance and industry designed to foster dialogue between North America and Europe. The climate between Western Europe and North America was marked by a certain manner of distrust and suspicion, owing to the then-burgeoning influence of post-WWII and Cold War politics on both sides. Seeking a way in which representatives could better establish diplomatic ties, organizer Jozef Retinger—a Polish political advisor then in exile from his native homeland by the Communist regime—sought to contact both top advisors and industry heads from other European nations, who in turn contacted then CIA-head Walter Bedell Smith and Eisenhower advisor Charles Douglas Jackson to lend their support. Subsequently, fifty delegates from 11 European countries and 11 delegates from the U.S. attended the first conference held at the Hotel de Bilderberg in the Netherlands from May 29-31 in 1954. The meetings were a rousing success, and soon became inaugurated as an annual conference held worldwide, with attendees now numbering between 120-150.

Retinger's background is worth noting, since his background during WWII remains unclear. It is clear that he met with top leaders of the Polish Underground who were then under Soviet annex in 1944. Yet certain factions viewed him with mistrust; was he working on behalf of German occupying forces? Allied forces? The then-exiled Prime Minister Wladyslaw Sikorski? The question remained unclear, and he survived several assassination attempts before his exile in 1947. What is known is that both Sikorski and Retinger were strong supporters of a European unification, and that the latter helped found both the Council of Europe (a concept which was wholeheartedly proposed and embraced by British Prime Minister—and Freemason—Winston Churchill as early as 1943) and the European Movement International between 1947 and 1949; both of which are direct precursors to the current European Union.

Briefly put, both organizations were strong promoters of the concept of a fully integrated and centralized "United States of Europe" in which a centralized European parliament and Constitution would be directly applicable to all citizens under its purview, regardless of which respective national region they dwelled in, each subject to applicable centralized law and edict. Enlisting various high-level industrialists and lobbyists and directly influencing United Nations decisions, these integrated European movements disseminated various think-tanks—including the

Bilderberg conferences— throughout the 1950s until 1993, when the Maastricht Treaty came into unanimous effect and the architects of a federalized Europe realized their dream some 50 years later with the emergence of the European Union.

The similarities between the EU and the concept of synarchy mentioned previously in this chapter are altogether striking. True, the former may not speak the mystical language of enlightened despotism (proposed as early as 370 BC by Plato in his *Republic*) guiding man's evolution through direct reign and control, but the notion of a singular law, a singular constitution, a singular government all betoken the same quest for omniscient power as predicted by D'Alveydre as early as 1887 (which owes more than a tip of the hat to the initial influence of a central federalized government proposed by the Masonic founding fathers of the U.S.) In fact, one can't help to think of the ghost of D'Alveydre smiling as he stood in line at the Euro Disney in 1992, knowing that his initial seed would come into full fruition less than one year later. Tyrants can be such thoughtfully patient gardeners at times, indeed.

These days, the heads and attendees of Bilderberg conferences have included owners from the Washington Post and New York Times; heads of IBM, Google, Unilever, Goldman Sachs, Nestle, BP and Barclays Bank; heads of the Federal Reserve Bank, the World Trade Organization, the Council on Foreign Relations and the Department of Defense; and even foreign royalty and presidents (in a largely symbolic gesture, we presume.) And yet despite this level of combined wealth and prestige, economic disparity both in the U.S. and internationally is at an all-time high; medical and disease-borne crises remain at critical levels; and the effective notion of high-level surveillance techniques has been proven not to be a flight of fancy, but an orchestrated tactic used by several governments—all of whom represent supposedly democratic interests.

And yet, these multinational corporations continue to see record profits, international tax loopholes, increased presence and a suspiciously high degree of lobbying influence. Wars are fought solely along broadly established economic lines, sanctions are placed into effect, and policies that directly affect public safety are implemented without public approval or knowledge.

With this in mind, shall we be so quick to rashly dismiss D'Alveydre as a crackpot?

Dangers of internationalist efforts

The dangers of both the Trilateral Commission and the Bilderberg group(s) are directly *because*, not in spite of, their supposed transparency. By operating in direct view of public scrutiny, they allege benevolence and diplomacy, inviting any casual observer to see for themselves what these meeting seek to accomplish.

Yet, despite this factor of transparency, both organizations remain rooted in an ideology that embraces a centralized and homogenous culture, both free of the nuances and diversity of traditional nation-states, but also fostering an "interdependence" on the sanctity and unassailability of a unified super-power, controlling each and every aspect of its subjects lives and prohibiting free speech, movement, exchange, dissenting opinion and autonomy by the establishment of universal power. In essence, the most successful realization of the Illuminati dream imaginable.

Members

As private organizations, it has only been until very recently that both the Trilateral Commission and the Bilderberg conferences have opened up membership lists to the public due to extreme scrutiny, largely based on their avowed issues of "security" and legal standings as private, non-profit entities.

Members of the Trilateral Commission have included: Shell Netherlands CEO Dick Benschop; Former National Intelligence Chairman Joseph Nye, Sr.; former Federal Reserve Chairmen Alan Greenspan and Paul Volcker; Mattel CEO Robert Eckert; U.S. Senators Dianne Feinstein, John D. Rockefeller IV and Charles Rangel; former Secretary of States Henry Kissinger and Madeline Albright; Hess CEO John A. Hess; former EU Ambassadors John Bruton, Tomas Hendrik Ilves and Max Jakobson; BAE Systems Chairman Richard Olver; NATO Chairman Pierre Lellouche; ING Vice Chairman Cees Maas; Bain & Company Managing Adviser Robin Buchanan; Atlantic Media Co. CEO David Bradley; Santander UK CEO Ana Patricia Botin; UBS Vice Chairman Lord Brittan of Spennithorne; Toyota Motor Co. Chairman Fujio Cho; Bank of Tokyo-

Mitsubishi President Nobuyuki Hirano; Samsung President Lee-jae Yong; Korean Ambassador Hong-Seok Hyun; AIG Vice Chairman Jakob Frankel; former Israeli Ambassador Itamar Rabinovich; SMS Chairman Heinrich Weiss; Prince Philip of Greece; Siemens CEO Philip Loscher; HSBC Director Rachel Lomax; N.M. Rothschild Advisor Panagis Vourloumis; former Executive Director of the 9/11 Commission on Terrorist Attacks Philip Zelikow; and former U.S. National Security and Intelligence Advisors Dennis Blair and James L. Jones.

Members and attendees of the Bilderberg conferences have included: Citigroup Vice Chairman Peter Orszag; AXA CEO Henri de Castries; Dow Chemical CEO Andrew Liveris; Queen Beatrix of the Netherlands; former US Congressman Richard "Dick" Gephardt; Former President Bill Clinton; U.S. Senators John Edwards, Dianne Feinstein, John Kerry and Sam Nunn; former Secretaries of State Henry Kissinger and Condoleeza Rice; Xerox CEO Paul Allaire; former BP CEO John P. Browne; Barclays CEO J. Martin Taylor; F.Hoffmann-LeRoche and Co. CEO Fritz Gerber; Former Director of N.M. Rothschild Norman Lamont; Central Europe Trust Chairman Andrzej

Olechowski; Goldman Sachs Chairman Peter Sutherland; Former U.S. Treasury Secretary Robert Rubin; Google Executive Chairman Eric Schmidt; Prince Philippe of Belgium; ALCOA CEO Klaus Kleinfeld; former World Bank Presidents Robert Zoellick and James Wolfenson; EU Ambassador Bjorn Grydeland; European Central Bank President Jean-Claude Trichet; Goldman Sachs CEO Peter Weinberg; Wall Street Journal Editor Robert Bartley; IBM Chairman Louis Gerstner, Jr.; TD Bank President Edmund W. Clark; Former U.S. Senator Tom Daschle; Merrill Lynch Vice Chairman Harold Ford, Jr.; Former Federal Reserve Chairman Ben Bernanke; National Security Agency Director Keith Alexander; Novartis Chairman Daniel Vasella; Amazon Founder and CEO Jeff Bezos; and Microsoft founder and CEO Bill Gates.

Chapter Six: COUNCIL ON FOREIGN RELATIONS

Since its founding in 1921, the Council on Foreign Relations has been one of the most prestigious think-tanks devoted to global economic and trade policies in history. Unlike other private entities (such as the Trilateral Commission or Bilderberg group), the Council on Foreign Relations has woven itself into the fabric of American society, becoming a deeply ingrained public informer and policy advisors most American citizens simply take for granted, never questioning how much influence this seemingly "private" entity has over both domestic and international politics.

Which might be precisely why this 5000-member private "think tank" is viewed with such suspicion by critical observers.

Few Americans can argue that issues of free trade, financial regulations and economic consolidations are at the forefront of the current U.S. economic system. But how are those policies constructed? Who or what informs them? Why is it U.S. voters get very little say in how policies which affect domestic jobs on the most critical level are implemented? Are these policies in the best interest of the American public? Or do they serve entities that have a much more specific interest in mind; an interest that serves not only global entities, but a wholesale global consolidation of power of which the U.S. represents only one very small aspect— and furthermore, one in which the interests of democracy play absolutely no role whatsoever?

In order to better examine the role that the Council has played within setting both domestic and international policies over the past 95 years, it's necessary to go back to the history of the Council and examine the pretext and context in which it was formed.

Origins of the Council on Foreign Relations

Immediately following the first World War, America faced a certain dilemma on its interaction with foreign nations, in particular Germany. America had been an initial supporter of Germany during its entrance into the war, but public and government sentiment soon turned against the nation, and support was at best ambivalent; and at worst, critical. After Germany's defeat, a fellowship of leading scholars, economists and political advisors had been asked to brief then-President Woodrow

Wilson (who had famously used the term 'New World Order' during his Fourteen Points speech of 1918 when he stated apropos of Germany's involvement in WWI: *"We wish her only to accept a place of equality among the peoples of the world – the new world in which we now live – instead of a place of mastery."*) about options of international diplomacy once the war had ended. At the conclusion of the delegates' participation in the Paris Peace Conference of 1919, they decided to create an Anglo-American private institution called The Institute of International Affairs, which would proffer an independent, non-partisan opinion on international relations. Yet the American public was wary of any internationalist activity as a result of the tragedies of WWI, and withdrew support in a wave of public outcry. The fellowship instead reconstituted under the name of the Council on Foreign Relations and began meeting discreetly to avoid arousing public suspicion until 1922, when they announced their formal incorporation.

Immediately prior to the outbreak of WWII, both the Ford, Rockefeller and Carnegie Foundations—all of whom have been noted as having distinct ties to the Illuminati, with the Rockefellers serving as the chief "bloodline"—

began funding the Council, leading to the establishment of various sub-committees which served to influence both local and national leaders, and subsequently public opinion about growing concerns and threats to international diplomacy. Eventually, the Council's esteem within the federal government became so great that during the outbreak of WWII they were asked to be strategic advisors on economic, military and political imperatives facing America's entry into the war. Their prominence within key strategic initiatives of the U.S. Government continued to last through the Cold War and Vietnam (a survey of over 500 government officials conducted between 1945 and 1972 indicated that well over 50% were serving or had served as key members of the Council) up until this very day. Which hastens to ask, why would a private, independent, non-partisan membership organization have such a key and decisive influence over economic, political and military initiatives?

Perhaps most prescient are the words of former Supreme Court Justice Felix Frankfurter, who stated at the height of the Council's disproportionate representation in the U.S. government during WWII and the Cold War:

"The real rulers in Washington are invisible and exercise power from behind the scenes."

Criticism of the Council on Foreign Relations

The Council has been praised by media and political luminaries such as Brian Williams, Fareed Zakaria, Senator Chuck Hagel and the actress Angelina Jolie (whose qualifications as a credible source on international policy were obviously so well-established that the Council solicited her membership in 2007) who have gone on record as stating that the Council is an *"indispensable resource in an increasingly complex world."* which is much of what you'd expect from paid Council members; which, in fact, all four are. When former Secretary of State (and both Trilateral Commission, Bilderberg participant, long-running Council chairman and alleged high-ranking Illuminati member) Henry Kissinger was recently asked to comment about the 2008 CFR-sponsored Global Governance Program (which calls for a reconceptualization of national sovereignty, citing the EU's consolidation of sovereignty as a guiding model; is the previous chapter still in the back of your mind yet?), he commented: *"it will give new impetus to American foreign policy... I think the task will be to develop an overall strategy for America in this period when, really, a new world order can be created. It's a great opportunity..."*

Not surprisingly, the name of David Rockefeller rears his head again as Council Chairman and major funder)—this time, in a 1991 speech when he stated: *"We are grateful to the Washington Post, the New York Times and other great publications whose directors have attended our meetings and respected the promises of discretion for almost forty years. It would have been impossible for us to develop our plan for the world if we had been subject to the bright lights of publicity during those years. But the world is now more sophisticated and prepared to march towards a world-government. The supranational sovereignty of an intellectual elite and world bankers is surely preferable to the National auto-determination practiced in past centuries."*

Even earlier in 1974, in an issue of the Council's publication *Foreign Affairs*, a Council member was even less selective in describing overall Council goals implicitly, stating: *"The New World Order will have to be built from the bottom up rather than from the top down...but in the end run around national sovereignty eroding it piece by piece will accomplish much more than the old fashioned frontal assault."*

And perhaps most damningly was the outburst from Council member James Warburg, son of Council co-founder and Federal Reserve architect Paul Warburg, when stating before the U.S. Senate Committee on Foreign Relations on February 17, 1950: *"We shall have world government, whether you like it or not. The only question is whether world government will be by conquest or consent."*

So much for impartial, independent and bipartisan analysis. But what of criticism from independent sources?

Judge Advocate General of the U.S. Navy and former Council on Foreign Relations member for over 16 years, Chester Ward, explains his disavowal for the Council, citing its existence as a "shadow government" thusly: *"The most powerful clique in these elitist groups have one objective in common; they want to bring about the surrender of the sovereignty of the national independence of the United States. A second clique of international members in the CFR comprises Wall Street international bankers* and their key agents. *Primarily, they want the world banking monopoly from whatever power ends up in the control of global government... Once the ruling members of the CFR shadow government have decided that the U.S. Government should adopt a particular policy the very substantial research facilities of (the) CFR are put to work to develop arguments intellectual and emotional to support the new policy and to confound and discredit intellectually and politically any opposition. The main purpose of the Council on Foreign Relations is promoting the disarmament of U.S. sovereignty and national independence and submergence into an all powerful one world government."*

Another former Council member (and mentor to current Council member and former President Bill Clinton) was Georgetown University professor, political theorist and noted historian Carroll Quigley, who stated the matter more succinctly in his 1966 book *Tragedy and Hope:* "*The CFR is the American Branch of a society which originated in England, and which believes that national boundaries should be obliterated, and a one-world rule established.*"

Even earlier in 1962, former FBI agent Dan Smoot specifically referred to the Council by the title of his book *The Invisible Government*, citing that: *"The ultimate aim of the CFR is to create a one-world socialist system, and to make the U.S. an official part of it."*

Dangers of the Council on Foreign Relations

In keeping with the central focus, both historically and current, of this book, the Council on Foreign Relations represents one thread in a many tangled web of entities that seek the creation of a centralized world economic super-power, ruled neither by the democratic interests of its citizens nor their democratically-elected leaders, but by an international conglomerate of industry moguls, media figureheads, trans-national corporations and elected global political leaders who seek absolute authority and absolute control over the exchange of finance, media and thought. To this end, key Council initiatives, such as the implementation of NAFTA under Council member and then-President Bill Clinton (which benefited only those corporations large enough to buy into intercontinental trade and subjected three separate nations to a totalitarian restriction of economic Social Darwinism in practice) and the European Union (itself a product of Bilderberg architect Jozef Retinger) were established, lulling millions of Americans into a pipe-dream of greater material prosperity and alleged "security" while all the while tightening its grip around their collective throat. The danger of the Council is that so many citizens refuse to acknowledge it as anything more than an established pattern in the American fabric of life.

Members

Members of the Council on Foreign Relations have included: Former Director of U.S. Policy Planning Richard Haas; Federal Reserve Bank President Michael Moskow; former U.S. Ambassadors Morris Abramowitz, Walter Roberts and George Kennan; media mogul Oprah Winfrey; National Security Advisor Stewart Baker; 9/11 Commission Chairman Thomas Kean; Senators Sam Nunn, Jay Rockefeller and Joseph Lieberman; Fox Media CEO Rupert Murdoch; Former Vice Presidents Gerald Ford, Dick Cheney and Al Gore; former CIA Directors Allen Dulles and General David Petraeus; media pundit William F. Buckley; former Foreign Affairs Advisor William Bundy; Joint Chief of Staff Chairman Colin Powell;

billionaire investor George Soros; Former Secretaries of State Warren Christopher, Madeleine Albright and Condoleeza Rice; ABC Television CEO Thomas Murphy; Television news anchors Tom Brokaw, Bill Moyers and Barbara Walters; Exxon CEO Lee Raymond; Former New Jersey State Governor Christine Todd Whitman; Coca-Cola CEO Muhtar Kent; Boeing CEO Donna Hrinak; educator and literary scholar Henry Louis Gates, Jr.; Former U.S. Secretary of Treasury Richard Rubin; United Nations co-founder Alger Hiss; Disney President Michael Ovitz; Former Secretary of Labor George P. Schultz; Former Massachusetts Governor William Weld; and former U.S. Secretary of Homeland Security Janet Napolitano.

Chapter Seven: SKULL & BONES

The college fraternity. The beloved staple of sophomoric comedic farces for the past fifty years. A collegiate staple, synonymous with good-natured hell-raising, wacky pranks and hi-jinks, hazing rituals and veritable wading pools of cheap beer. Through a fraternity, a student is expected to find brotherhood, camaraderie and forge the establishment of personal and business connections which are bound to serve him throughout his professional life. A trait not at all unlike the purpose of numerous other non-educational fraternities, from the local Rotary Club to the Freemasons; perhaps dating as far back as the establishment of trade guilds in the Middle Ages.

Yet more recently, the institution of the college fraternity has come under pressure, with examples of alcoholism, physical and verbal abuse, sexual assault and racism cited by detractors seeking to demonize the beloved American figure of the "frat boy" into nothing more than a slovenly, ignorant and perpetually drunken wastrel frittering away his parents funding in an ocean of self-serving crudity, sloth and nightly keg parties.

If all fraternities bore the stigma of Yale University's Skull & Bones, perhaps these detractors might find something even more troublesome than the above-mentioned allegations.

What is it about Skull & Bones that strikes both fear and silence in all but the most casual observer? Is it the death-obsessed emblems surrounding so much of their fantastic lore, including rumors of harboring the mortal remains of some of America's most beloved heroes? Is it the tight-lipped secrecy that surrounds the group, so much that questioning rumors of affiliation has resulted in more than a handful of job firings? Or is it a historically traceable connection between its members and the upper echelons of international power, a power that has grafted itself by dint of affiliation to key leadership positions in the very same groups we have been covering to date?

After all, it's just a harmless college fraternity, isn't it? All good fun and games, if slightly more morbid than most. *Animal House* (whose Omega Theta Pi chapter allegedly takes their inspiration from Skull & Bones) in a sombre Halloween drag.

Read on, and you may find yourself grateful that binge drinking and a sliding GPA might be the biggest worries about your son while he's away at school.

Origins of Skull & Bones

Technically, the Skull & Bones society is not an undergraduate fraternity. Membership is by invitation only, and only extended to 15 inductees a year, and for that solely within their junior year. Furthermore, both current and historical membership rosters are kept completely private. There is no official mission statement for the Skull & Bones society, and the organization refuses to divulge their activities. Nor are their assets managed by Yale University, but by a private trust known as the Russell Trust Association (named after their co-founder and incorporated in 1856.) In fact, for many years both the society as well as Yale University refused to acknowledge the very existence of the group.

The Skull & Bones society was founded in 1832 as 'The Order of Skull & Bones'—or 'Bones' as it is informally referred to as—by Yale students William Huntington Russell and future U.S. Secretary of War and Freemason Alphonso

Taft (father of President William Howard Taft—who, in keeping with family tradition was himself both a Skull & Bones member as well as a Freemason.) It is uncertain the purpose behind the design of the group—allegedly it was after a dispute over that years Phi Beta Kappa awards, although it seems more likely it was established much like how many fraternities are established; as a mutual aid society of undergraduates banding together for fellowship and companionship. Albeit with strict criteria—in 1882, at least four prospective candidates had to be selected from student publications and at least four others had to be selected from captains of Yale's sporting teams—and a much more ghoulish motif than most.

Equally enigmatic is their famed emblem; a skull and bones underneath which is emblazoned the mysterious numerical legend 322. One suggestion is that the skull and bones represent the oath of mortality that recruits are sworn to keep silent, while the numbers represent the year and the initial two founders. Other, perhaps far-fetched, theories have included that the skull is an allusion to the famed head of 'Baphomet' allegedly idolized by the Knights Templar while the bones represent the shape of the cross upon which Roman emperor Constantine was crucified upon. Others claim the numbers refer to the death of famed Greek orator Demosthenes, to a complex numerical code having magical significance (it is worth noting that the skull and crossbones motif is found in numerous other secret societies from the Knights of Pythias to the "Chamber of Reflection" found in Masonic initiations.)

The Skull & Bones Hall is referred to as "The Tomb" and bears considerable Egyptian and Greek influence upon its facade. Entrance into the Tomb is strictly forbidden to non-members, although it has been referred to as "something like a German beer hall," with bizarre passageways, imposing statues of knights in armor and a mysterious chamber replete with candles, coffins, skeletons, a chopping block, bats and a basin containing a red fluid. In this chamber, candidates have been known to be divested of metal jewelry (a trait common to all Masonic initiations) where they are placed into the coffin, 'chanted' over, and 'reborn' again into society where they are given a robe embroidered with arcane symbols. A bone with the candidate's name engraved upon it is then thrown into a heap of other bones, symbolizing his or her (Yale became a co-ed campus in 1969, although the Skull & Bones society refused to accept female members until a lawsuit in 1991) link to the fraternity, which is hauled out at the initiation of each and every meeting. The candidate is then given a secret name, often of mythological, historical or literary import— examples being Hamlet, Thor, Shakespeare, Sancho Panza, Baal, Magog or the distinctly Masonic Boaz—with which he or she will be known to as other members. They are also expected to complete a detailed, two-night description of his sexual activity and autobiography, fears and motivations at some point in the coming year, lending on the all the more incongruous appearance of an encounter group session to the already bizarre atmosphere.

Controversy of Skull & Bones

Critics are quick to point out that the activity of a student-sponsored privately run "society" based on exclusivist principles—which leans heavily towards White Protestant males—on university grounds is at odds with the inclusivist nature of the modern American educational system. This however, is nothing more than a straw man argument for the dangers which burrow beneath this garish and grotesque melange of high privilege and entitlement.

As early as 1873, allegations were being lodged against the group (who informally call themselves 'Bonesmen') that they were made privy to student funds directed to the University for their own usage and that there was a disproportionate tendency for its alumni to be selected for key positions in finance over other Yale graduates. More serious criminal charges have been lodged against the group, alleging that grave-robbing was a regular initiation practice for prospective candidates and that the group currently houses the remains of Apache leader Geronimo (it is widely held that U.S. Senator and known Bonesman Prescott Bush—father and grandfather of future presidents George H.W. Bush and George W. Bush respectively, themselves also known Skull & Bones members—was responsible for the theft), former President Martin van Buren and Mexican revolutionary Pancho Villa.

Still others have lodged the allegations that rape and kidnapping are also commonplace initiatory trials prospective candidates are expected to undertake in order to prove both their worthiness as well as their identifiably "elite" natures as future leaders in the fields of politics and industry by placing themselves outside the confines of the law, silencing their victims with immeasurably deep funds. *"Rape is so commonplace on campuses to begin with,"* alleges one victim, *"that even on Yale you're going to find it. But with Bonesmen it's different. They truly think they're above the law. And with all the money that floats in and out of the Tomb, you start wonder maybe that really is the case."* Or, as one former member put it in a 1977 article, *"It's like trying to look into the Mafia. Remember, they're a secret society, too."*

However, allegations and hearsay are one thing. Proven claims—based not on conjecture, but verifiable documentation—reveal a curious web of nepotism and cronyism that unquestionably link Skull & Bones to other groups previously covered in this book, confirming the group's reputation of manipulation, favoritism and exclusivity.

One of the co-founders of the Council on Foreign Relations was Secretary of State under Theodore Roosevelt Elihu Root. While serving as a state attorney, Root hired a Bonesman named Henry Stimson to serve on his council. Stimson later went on to serve as Secretary of War under fellow Bonesman William Howard Taft, and eventually Secretary of State under

Herbert Hoover—himself a co-founder of the Council on Foreign Relations. Stimson was eventually nominated as Secretary of War a second time, serving under two presidents— Franklin Delano Roosevelt (whose links to the Illuminati were explored in Chapter Three) and Harry S. Truman (a known Freemason)—during America's entry into World War II, where he was one of the leading advocates not only for war against Germany but also the construction of the atomic bomb.

Stimson's point man for the Pentagon for the Manhattan Project (which oversaw the development of the atomic bomb) was a fellow Bonesman named Harvey Hollister Bundy. Bundy's two sons, William and McGeorge—both also notable members of Skull & Bones—later went on to serve key roles as CIA and foreign affairs advisors to Presidents Kennedy and Johnson during America's entrance into the Vietnam conflict. Not surprisingly, both also went on to hold key roles in the Council on Foreign Relations (William Bundy was editor of the Council's publication *Foreign Affairs*, and was noted for once stating that the *"role of government is to stimulate a mass-scale change in attitude."*) It may be no coincidence that McGeorge Bundy was later to serve as President of the Ford Foundation, whose links to the Trilateral Commission, the Council on Foreign Relations and the Illuminati have been ably documented already.

The Stimson-Bundy family link isn't the only hereditary link in the Skull & Bones chain to worm its way through the upper levels of political, military and defense intrigue. For that, we need only observe the curious relationship between the Harriman family (of international bankers Brown Brothers and Harriman fame) and the political dynasty of the Bush family. A link, curiously enough that had ties to both the regimes of Nazi Germany and the Communist USSR—both allegedly, "enemies" of American interests.

Brown Brothers Harriman—currently the oldest and largest private bank in the U.S.—was formed after the merger of two entities, Brown & Brothers and A.W. Harriman & Co. in 1931. The founding partners of this merger included 8 members of Skull & Bones, most notably Prescott Bush (who we have already been introduced to) and future Ambassador to the U.S.S.R, W. Averell Harriman. In 1942, an executive order signed by President Roosevelt seized the property of Prescott Bush, who also served as Director for the Union Banking Company of New York, under charges of 'trading with the national enemy.'

The reason for the seizure was that Union Banking was also *the* asset clearing and holding house for German steel magnate Fritz Thyrssen, which had been funding Hitler since 1924. Inexplicably, Prescott Bush went on to be elected U.S. State Senator, later claiming responsibility for launching Richard Nixon's into politics (Nixon's links to David Rockefeller have been amply detailed, to mention nothing of the role Secretary of State Henry Kissinger has played in numerous groups detailed elsewhere in this book) and, coincidentally, serving as the first treasurer on the national campaign for Planned Parenthood in 1947 (whose links to the Van Duyn bloodline of the Illuminati were explored in Chapter Three.) We'll go over the exploits of Prescott's Skull & Bones legacy-carriers, George H.W. and George W., shortly but for now, let's turn our attentions back to one W. Averell Harriman.

As mentioned earlier, Harriman served as U.S. Ambassador to the U.S.S.R under President Truman. Yet prior to this, the company that Harriman formed, Brown Brothers Harriman, also owned the previously mentioned Union Banking. During his tenure as U.S.S.R Ambassador, Harriman was responsible not only for maintaining relatively cordial relations with Stalin, but also shipping entire factories into Russia. Upon his return to the U.S., Harriman began working closely with the Council on Foreign Relations, despite being adamantly referred to as a Soviet spy by former KGB Major-turned-defector Anatoliy Golitsyn. Some research recently uncovered also indicates that Harriman may have had a direct role in the transfer of nuclear plans and U.S. dollar printing plates to Soviet Russia during the Cold War.

One of Brown Brothers Harriman's directors was Robert Lovett, himself a Bonesman. Lovett was a chief advisor to Truman regarding the re-organization of American intelligence agencies immediately following World War II. It was at Lovett's insistence that the CIA was formed in 1947, and the agency was soon populated by such a disproportionate number of Skull & Bones members that Yale Professor of History Gaddis Smith was once prompted to remark, *"Yale has influenced the Central Intelligence Agency more than any other university, giving the CIA the atmosphere of a class reunion."*

One CIA-operated project was the notorious MK-ULTRA; a covert psychological operations experiment during the 1950s and 1960s, the full extent of which we are still uncovering to this day. The project entailed the use of powerful psychotropic drugs, isolation chambers, brainwashing techniques and other methods of psychological manipulation and control (much of it administered at mental institutions such as Bridgewater State Hospital in Massachusetts), and was financed by and large by the "independent" H. Richardson Foundation; a foundation established by one Eugene Stetson, an Assistant Director under Prescott Bush, and a Skull & Bones alumni himself.

Other alumni from the Skull & Bones roster filling the ranks of the CIA have included F. Trubee Davison (CIA Personnel Director starting in 1951), William Sloane Coffin, Jr. (CIA agent, 1950-1953), William Francis Buckley (CIA agent 1956-1970, Station Chief in Beirut 1983-1985), Hugh Cunningham (CIA agent 1950-1973), Charles Whitehouse (CIA agent 1947-1956 and U.S. Ambassador to Laos and Thailand in the 1970s; a time that coincidentally saw a substantial rise in heroin trafficking from that region);Dino Pionzio (CIA Station Chief in Santiago Chile 1970-1975; a time that coincidentally saw the overthrow of the Allende regime by a bloody coup d'etat and its replacement by the notoriously bloodthirsty Augusto Pinochet), former U.S. Senator David Boren (CIA Committee member 1985-1999), and, of course, future President George H.W. Bush (CIA Director 1976-1977).

There is considerable controversy regarding Bush's tenure in the CIA. Uncovered evidence indicates that he may have been involved as early as 1963, in particular with a counter-intelligence unit code-named 'Pegasus' implicated in a potential plot to assassinate President Kennedy according to transcripts of tapes obtained from a tap on the phone of FBI Director J. Edgar Hoover; transcripts which include the names of Hoover, future Vice President (and brother of David) Nelson Rockefeller, CIA Director (and Council on Foreign Relations Director) Allen Dulles, and one "George Bush" of the CIA. Both Bush and the CIA have implicitly denied the allegations of the existence of both Pegasus and Bush's involvement prior to his nomination as Director in 1976; which, as an intelligence agency responsible for disambiguation of both information and misinformation, naturally befits a secret organization.

One thing is for certain; the invocation of a 'New World Order' raised many an eyebrow when Bush delivered his famed address before congress on September 11, 1990 (exactly 11 years prior to the date of the 9/11 attacks on the World Trade Center; a date forever ingrained with many Americans as the rationale behind Bush's son George W.'s entrance into the Afghanistan conflict and subsequent war on Iraq.) In it, the senior Bush justified his invasion of Iraq precipitation the Persian Gulf Crisis of 1990-1992 with the following words:

"A new partnership of nations has begun, and we stand today at a unique and extraordinary moment. The crisis in the Persian Gulf, as grave as it is, also offers a rare opportunity to move toward an historic period of cooperation. Out of these troubled times, our fifth objective—a new world order—can emerge: A new era—free from the threat of terror, stronger in the pursuit of justice and more secure in the quest for peace... America and the world must defend common vital interests. And we will... Americans have stepped forward to share a tearful goodbye with their families before leaving for a strange and distant shore. At this very moment, they serve together with Arabs, Europeans, Asians and Africans in

defense of principle and the dream of a new world order. That is why they sweat and toil in the sand and the heat and the sun."

The 'New World Order' is, of course, a phrase most commonly associated with the Illuminati. And it is equally indicative of the ultimate goal of all globalist and international institutions who strive to forge a new era; perhaps one of peace, justice and prosperity. But only *to those who can afford it.*

There have been approximately 7,000 U.S. casualties to date resulting from both the Persian Gulf Crisis of 1990-1991, and the ongoing US Wars on Afghanistan and Iraq since 2001. How many were lost for "*the quest of peace*"; and how many were lost for the sake of a 'New World Order'?

Dangers of Skull & Bones

It is all too tempting to view Skull & Bones as a breeding ground for future recruits into the Illuminati or conversely, more overt societies such as the Trilateral Commission, the Council on Foreign Relations or even (as amply demonstrated by this chapter) the CIA. It seems that given the vast links and behavior of Skull &

Bones alumni, one would be hard-pressed to find an outfit more smug about their elitism, secrecy and implication in a tangled web of conspiracy and duplicity at the highest levels of American political intrigue; a smugness and arrogance the organization has done little to dispel in the 180-plus years of their existence.

During the Regent degree of the Illuminati, the candidate, after being directed to a skeleton, is asked *"Whether there lies the body of a king, nobleman, or beggar?"* His expected answer is that *"The character of being a man is the only one that is of importance."*

The legend engraved on the inner chamber of the Skull & Bones Tomb reads: *"Wer war der Thor, wer Weiser, Bettler oder Kaiser? Ob Arm, ob Reich, im Tode gleich."*

A rough translation of which is, *"Who was the fool, who the wise man, beggar or king? Whether poor or rich, all's the same in death."*

Members

In addition to the previously named parties, other members of Skull & Bones have included: investment banker and founder of Morgan Stanley Harold Stanley; *Time-Life* magazine founder Henry Luce (a member of the Council on Foreign Relations); NY Mets co-founder (and uncle of George H.W. Bush) George Herbert Walker, Jr.; writer Archibald MacLeish; Banker and Dean Witter founder Dean Witter, Jr.; former Senator and Heinz heir H. John Heinz; Secretary of State John Kerry; former Federal Reserve chairman Pierre Jay; co-founder of the Council on Foreign Relations Charles Seymour; publisher, creator of the *Fortune 500* Russell Davenport (also a member of the Council on Foreign Relations); former Senators John Patton Jr., James Buckley, John Chafee and Victor Ashe; Sears Chairman Edward Lampert; FedEx founder Frederick Wallace Smith; former U.S. Ambassadors David Thorne, Winston Lord, Evan Galbraith and James Jeremiah Wadsworth; *National Review* founder William F. Buckley, Jr.; Cornell University co-founder Andrew Dickson White; and U.S. Trust President Daniel Davison.

Chapter Eight: THE COMMITTEE OF 300

So far to date, we have chosen to examine secret societies that are rooted in incontrovertible historical evidence. Other examples of secret societies throughout history, such as the White Dragon Society, the Order of Nine Angels, the Knights of the Golden Circle, the Esoteric Order of Dagon and the Order of the Palladium and the Four Pi Society mentioned in this book's introduction, have been omitted either because their existence has been proven to be a hoax, evidence for their existence is tenable at best or their influence is so marginal as to have virtually no effect whatsoever on the world at large.

When it comes to the Committee of 300, we are straddling the line between fiction, exaggeration and historical possibility.

In literature pertaining to secret societies and conspiracy theories, the Committee of 300 is sometimes overlooked or understated. Certain researchers simply assume that the Committee is simply another code-name for Illuminati, and use it interchangeably. Still others have pointed out critical flaws in existing theories behind the Committee's existence, such as texts which have proven to be forgeries. Still others have meticulously pieced together historical evidence that links many of the figures we have discussed to date with the alleged origins of the Committee itself; and it is this last factor that is of particular interest to us.

The correlation between industrialization, media communication, economic control and globalization has been amply demonstrated throughout history, and was present even as early as the dawn of the Industrial Revolution in the 18th century (coincidentally, a period that saw the rise of both Freemasonry and the Illuminati.) Parallel to this has been an increase in global population growth, which British economist and scholar Thomas Malthus predicted as early as 1798 would ultimately result in what has come to be known as a 'Malthusian catastrophe'; in which both natural causes, such as famine, starvation and disease as well as artificial constructs such as war, poverty and violence would be inevitable conclusions that were fundamentally cyclical results necessary to redress this expansion in population growth when faced with a scarcity of resources. The reason this highly controversial conclusion is brought up here is not just to reinvigorate long-dormant economic theories, but so the reader will have a bit of context when addressing the plausibility of certain long-scale plans of the Committee of 300.

World population statistics indicate that the 2014 global census was estimated at roughly 7 Billion people. The World Health Organization predicts an incremental increase of approximately 10% every 5 years; meaning that by 2029, we could be facing a global population of 9 Billion. With both global economic disparity at an all-time high, crises of food shortages, incessant and transglobal conflicts and the spread of highly contagious viral diseases such as Ebola, the question isn't whether or not Malthus was right, but whether or not we can afford not to entertain the ramifications of the existence of the Committee of 300?

Origins of the Committee of 300

Generally speaking, many theorists attribute the Committee of 300 to a quote from murdered German industrialist Walther Rathenau in a 1909 article when he stated, *"Three hundred men, all of whom known one another, direct the economic destiny of continents and choose their successors from among themselves."* At the time, Germany was facing an unprecedented increase in national wealth, and subsequently, a marked increase in both the cost of living and contrast between both labor and leisure classes; a discrepancy not helped by Kaiser Wilhelm II's contentious relations with distant nations as well as his diplomatic support with neighboring countries, which precipitated Germany's entrance into WWI in 1914. This discrepancy, which saw an increase in wealth for only a few of the nation's 15 million residents, found an immediate target through anti-semitism, which had been a hallmark of German culture since the Middle Ages.

By 1912, journalists such as Theodor Fritsch declared Rathenau's statement an "*open confession of indubitable Jewish hegemony*" (Rathenau was indeed of Jewish origin) and relied upon the previous century's apocryphal *Protocols of the Learned Elders of Zion*—a document since proven to be a hoax—as testimonial evidence of a global Jewish conspiracy. Despite Rathenau's insistence that the three hundred leaders he referred to were industry leaders and not necessarily Jews (and clarified that he abhorred the ramifications of such exclusivity), the industrialist was assassinated by three accomplices in 1922, one of whom, Erwin Kern, explicitly cited Rathenau's membership in the "300 Elders of Zion" as rationale for the murder.

Still, others trace the existence of the Committee not to early 20th century Germany, but all the way back to 1727 and the emergence of a mysterious "Council of 300" orchestrated by the British East India Trading Company.

The East India Trading Company was a private trading company that was actually officially chartered by Queen Elizabeth I as early as 1600 (it is worth noting that a constant strategic advisor to the Queen was Sir John Dee, a noted purveyor of Hermetic and Rosicrucian doctrines.) The company's primary focus was within the Indian subcontinent and the Chinese mainland, where it rose to account for more than half the world's trade, importing silks, teas, dyes—and most notably, gunpowder and opium. These trades may have indeed been the business model for such modern day clandestine operations as the Mafia and various Central and South American drug cartels.

The company's shares were owned by various wealthy British merchants and aristocrats, and was only indirectly controlled by the British government, who owned no shares. This may be the first instance of a private company holding more executive power and wealth over trade and exchange than its own government, but it would be far from the last. It just so happened that many of these merchants and aristocrats belonged not only to the chivalric Order of the Garter (one of the highest and most prestigious honors to be bestowed upon a non-monarchic British subject, and itself a semi-secret society which is the cause of much speculation), but also Freemasonry and various Masonic offshoots, such as the Order of the Scarlet Cord, the Red Cross of Constantine, and the Order of St. John of Jerusalem. It is from the latter (an offshoot of the Knights of Malta, which in turn claims direct lineage from the Knights Templar) that the core of the Council of 300 was alleged to have formed, primarily as an exclusive trade committee made up of only the most elite and high-ranking European (for at this point, the founding members of the Council had turned mercenary and established negotiations and alliances with other European trading unions, such as the Dutch, French and Portuguese East India Companies and the Barbary Company) merchants and noblemen of only the highest wealth. It was rumored that this Council had exclusive control of over 300 ports; hence the title, Council of 300. Inevitably, these strands

144

were to weave their way into the fabric of the Illuminati; where they were to weave their way into even more disparate societies and institutions.

The British East India Trading Company was formally dissolved in 1874, largely as a result of British colonization of India (which many theorists believe to be largely the result of a Council of 300 plot.) Competitive maritime trade was rapidly declining, both as a result of industry saturation as well as the rise of inter-European continental trade owing to quicker means of transport, such as the railroad. Yet the Council of 300 had already established themselves as an unassailable and omnipresent mercantile force, whose numbers had now grown to some 300 families, individuals and institutions. Some of the more significant among the latter included the Bank of London, NM Rothschild, Standard Oil (established by Rockefeller patriarch John D. Rockefeller), De Beers Diamond and Mining Co. (established by Cecil Rhodes) and Barclays Bank—all of which have had figures associated with and closely intertwined elsewhere in this book.

Informally, it is said that the Council refers to themselves as "the Olympians," owing to their identification with the gods of Greek myth.

It is one thing to wield omniscient power in the fields of industry. But true power comes from domination of the political sphere. If Freemasonry and the Illuminati have taught us anything, it is that both politics, industry and an ulterior agenda hidden and plotted behind impenetrable veils of secrecy have made for some of the most successful bedfellows in history. Even unsuccessful political candidates such as Mitt Romney and Donald Trump—both of whom began their political careers after achieving inordinate success in the spheres of finance and real estate—are aware of this. The key factor then, is how to achieve political strength subtly and unobtrusively? The answer is through the manipulation of public attitudes by the dissemination of information. The media. To this end, the Council established both non-profit think tanks and worldwide conglomerates with political aims. Included among some of the more influential ones are the following four:

1.) Chatham House, the Royal Institute of Affairs. A private, non-governmental agency headquartered in London established in 1920, who claims their mission is "*to help build a sustainably secure, prosperous and just world*" by "*engaging governments, the private sector, civil society and its members in open debate and confidential discussion on the most significant developments in international affairs.*" In actuality, the Royal Institute of Affairs was established by Lionel Curtis, a staunch British federalist who worked alongside the Council of Foreign Relations during its development. Curtis was one of the direct descendants of the founding core of the Council of 300, and worked extensively with Illuminati member and Freemason Cecil Rhodes towards the expansion of British colonization in Africa. In reality, Chatham House has worked extensively to disseminate views calling for British unity and expansion as well as publishing reports in favor not only of a fully integrated European Union, but has also worked to establish stricter regulations ensuring a centralized constitution.

2.) The Council on Foreign Relations, whom we've already gone over in detail during Chapter Six.

3.) The Club of Rome. A global think tank founded in 1968 by Aurelio Peccei and Alexander King in Rome (now headquartered in Switzerland), the Club of Rome purports *"to act as a global catalyst for change through the identification and analysis of the crucial problems facing humanity and the communication of such problems to the most important public and private decision makers as well as to the general public."* The Club first came to prominence in 1972 with a publication entitled *The Limits to Growth*, a Malthusian document which argued that the limits of economic growth were contingent on rapidly dwindling resources—in particular oil; hence growth was subject to scarcity and in inverse proportion to demand (a notion which presaged the Oil Crisis of 1973.) Peccei, a noted Italian industrialist, was a known Freemason with ties to Licio Gelli's 'Propaganda Due' lodge; King, a British chemist and environmental scientist, is reputed to come from a long line of British Illuminati backers, and has been known to work "independently" alongside both the Trilateral Commission and the council on Foreign Relations.

4.) The Tavistock Institute on Human Relations. A Rockefeller funded think tank formed in 1947, the Tavistock Institute describes its mission as *"dedicated to the study of human relations for the purpose of bettering working life and conditions for all humans within their organizations, communities and broader societies and to the influence of environment in all its aspects on the formation or development of human character or capacity."* In reality, the group is acutely adept as a social engineering mechanism that has worked closely with the CIA during the MK-ULTRA project. Both Henry Kissinger and Paul Warburg—both of whose relationship with the Rockefellers and the Council on Foreign Relations we have covered elsewhere in this book— were early funders of Tavistock projects, and indeed, the Institute has worked closely in tandem with the Council on Foreign Relations for many years now. One of the founding members of the Tavistock, psychiatrist John Rawlings

Rees, made this revealing quote about the dynamic of social engineering during this 1940 speech before the National Conference on Mental Health: *"We can therefore justifiably stress our particular point of view with regard to the proper development of the human psyche, even though our knowledge be incomplete. We must aim to make it permeate every educational activity in our national life.... Public life, politics and industry should all of them be within our sphere of influence.... If we are to infiltrate the professional and social activities of other people, we must imitate the Totalitarians and organize some kind of fifth column activity."*

Goals of the Committee of 300

All secret societies must have an underlying agenda, and the Committee of 300 is no different. Some theorists have chosen to tack on all manner of far-fetched theories onto them, presenting them as a conglomerate of evil of superhuman proportions; others have chosen to present rational, clearly-thought out objectives. What we are concerned with in this work is verifiable evidence, and so we have chosen to select only a specific few:

1.) A One World Government with a singular currency, singular police/military force and absolute and unquestionable authority. This is the singular strand that connects all groups we have discussed to date.

2.) The abolition of national identity, as tantamount to the formation of a singular world-state.

3.) Establishment of technological advancements (described by Brzezinski in his book *Between Two Ages*) in mind and populace control. This is the real rationale by the establishment of think-tanks such as the Tavistock and Chatham House; to mold public opinion and engineer changes in social structure to allow greater susceptibility towards Committee-constructed initiatives.

4.) To bring about the end to all industrialization and the production of nuclear generated electric power in what is known as "the post-industrial zero-growth society". As noted earlier, the influence of Malthus looms large within the sphere of power wielded by the Committee, and the dissemination of zero-population growth was widely disseminated by the Club of Rome, whose founder Aurelio Peccei has been quoted as saying, *"Why should I concern myself with how many die? Even the Christian Bible says what is man that God should be mindful of him? For me men are nothing but a brain at one end and a shit factory at the other."*

5.) To suppress all scientific and medical development except for those deemed beneficial by the Committee. Especially targeted is nuclear energy for peaceful purposes. In an era in which greater funding for feasible energy solutions, medical discoveries and biotech research is at an all time high, the ongoing slew of world health and energy crises has increased exponentially. That the collective efforts of energy and world health organizations have been unable to meet these crises gives significant thought to ponder.

6.) To cause, by means of limited wars in advanced countries, and starvation and diseases in the Third World countries, the death of three billion people by the year 2050. As an adjunct to points four and five, both the ongoing conflicts in Iraq and Afghanistan as well as the increase of Ebola and its transmission seem to indicate that this may very well be reachable over the next 30-40 years.

7.) To weaken the moral fiber of nations and demoralize workers in the labor class by creating mass unemployment. The labor and economic crises facing both America and the EU for much of the past eight years is largely the result of both predatory banking practices as well as corporate rapaciousness which sacrifices family over profit, skill over automation, and craft over mass production.

8.) To cause a total collapse of the world's economies, engendering political chaos. Riots, such as those that occurred in Greece, Italy and Spain in 2012, to say nothing of domestic tensions in the U.S., have and will continue to become common-place as more and more political efforts are forced into states of panic and adaptation to a rapidly volatile and changing climax.

9.) To take control of all foreign and domestic policies of the U.S. This is particularly cogent during a time in which "Super-PACs", lessened restrictions on lobbying and campaign financial contributions, and noted special interest funding is at an all time high.

10.) To give the fullest support to supranational institutions such as the United Nations, the International Monetary Fund (IMF), the Bank of International Settlements, the World Court, making local institutions less effective, by gradually phasing them out or bringing them under the mantle of the UN.

11.) To penetrate and subvert all governments, and work from within them to destroy the sovereign integrity of the nations represented by them.

12.) To organize a worldwide terrorist apparatus. The sudden rise of militant groups such as ISIS, al-Qaeda, Boko Haram and al-Shabaab are no accident. Their funding generally comes from government assistance (in the case of al-Qaeda, directly *from* the U.S. during the 1980s) and with a widespread network, including nations generally inimical to terrorist operations, the threat has never been more dire; nor will it appear to dissipate anytime soon.

Members

Reputed members of the Committee of 300 have included: King Abdullah II of Jordan; Anglo American PLC CEO Cynthia Carroll; British Prime Minister David Cameron; Fox Media CEO Rupert Murdoch; former French President Nicolas Sarkozy; Senator Joe Lieberman; former Federal Reserve Chairman Alan Greenspan; former British Prime Minister Tony Blair; Microsoft founder Bill Gates; former Vice President Al Gore; former U.S. Treasury Secretary Timothy Geithner; British Chancellor Ed Balls; Queen Beatrix of the Netherlands; economist Mervyn King; Federal Reserve President William C. Dudley; former British Prime Minister Margaret Thatcher; economist Paul Krugman; Senator Arlen Specter; Lloyds

TSB Director Jan du Plessis; Goldman Sachs President Gary Cohn; former Swiss National Bank Director Jean-Pierre Roth; Prince Charles of Wales; investor Warren Buffett; former de Beers Diamond & Mining Chairman Nicholas Oppenheimer; former International Monetary Fund director Dominique Strauss-Kahn; former Federal Reserve Chairman Paul Volcker; Duke Edward of Kent; economist George Soros; Fiat Chairman John Philip Elkann; former World Trade Organization General Director Pascal Lamy; former Microsoft CEO Steve Ballmer; Banco Safra founder Moises Safra; Queen Elizabeth II; Matheson & Co. CEO James Sassoon; European Commission President Jean-Claude Juncker; Alfa-Bank Chairman Pyotr Aven; former U.S. SEC Chairman Arthur Levitt; Banque Nationale de Paris Chairman Michel Pebereau; former Bank of Italy Chairman Mario Draghi; and former European Central Bank Vice President Christian Noyer.

Chapter Nine: BOHEMIAN GROVE

Monte Rio. Snuggled deep into the woods of Sonoma County just overlooking the Russian River, this idyllic California hamlet of barely more than 1,000 residents is an ideal vacation getaway populated by dense forests of redwood trees and viaducts, lakes and streams. It's easy to lose yourself in the natural splendor of the surroundings, enraptured by the scenery and the warmly glowing Northern California nights, unaware that just a mile away, on a private 2,000 acre campground, some of the most powerful and elite leaders in world politics are gathered together to re-enact their ancient pagan forefathers' rites of drinking copiously and unrepentantly around a bonfire loomed over by a massive owl—the ancient Greco-Roman herald of knowledge and secrecy.

It's easy enough to perceive this highly-guarded two-week getaway as nothing more than a cabal of some of the most high level political magnates reaping their respective mid-life crises through a collegiate level weekend of alcohol-fueled high jinx draped in highly suggestive mythological motifs. It's as far removed from the daily life of the upper-class vacationing families nearby as the more sinister myth surrounding Bohemian Grove; those of sinister Luciferian rites lorded over by wealthy politicos hell-bent on world domination and infant sacrifice. It's tempting to think of the conversations between such turn of the century literati as Frank Norris and Jack London and statesmen such as Oliver Wendell Holmes and Theodore Roosevelt over an unending flask of undistilled moonshine, with only stale cigar smoke and Japanese lanterns summoning an eerie ambience in this preternatural landscape; but it's likely that such conversations belong to the hangovers of ghosts and rash hubris.

What is it about Bohemian Grove that invites such wild and far-fetched speculation? Other highly publicized weekend retreats for world politicos—such as Camp David or the G8 summit—rarely result in the sort of crazed allegations surrounding the Grove. Is it merely the garish "rites" that mark what would otherwise be seen as "blowing off steam" for overgrown frat boys accustomed to Brooks Brothers suits and bureaucratic spools of red tape that hold the lives of millions of Americans in their arthritic hands? Is it the vision of a naked Henry Kissinger leading a ghoulish coterie of Senators and industrial magnates around a bonfire to pay homage to an elite bloodline bestowed by the fortune of supernatural forces? Or is it that Bohemian Grove represents one in countless annual soirees among those very same names we've grown all-too-familiar with in the course of this book as being those which have an intimate link to the same threats of globalization and unswerving authority that have been amply demonstrated by this book over and over again?

A plaque directly outside the entrance to the campgrounds of Bohemian Grove bears a legend from Shakespeare's *A Midsummer Night's Dream* "Weaving Spiders Come Not Here." An ominous warning to would-be intruders that their fate could be the same as that of the humble spider; squashed and tossed out the window of a moving car into the rapids of the Russian River, lost to the rippling maw of nature? Or a knowing allusion to the myth of Arachne; that to penetrate the web of guarded secrets and defense will only result in an inescapable entanglement?

Despite successful attempts from researchers and documentary producers to break the spell of hermetic silence that surrounds the myth of Bohemian Grove, in the end only one neutral party knows—the Redwood trees. And they're not talking, either.

Origins of Bohemian Grove

"The Bohemian Grove, that I attend from time to time—the Easterners and the others come there—but it is the most faggy goddamned thing you could ever imagine, that San Francisco crowd that goes in there; it's just terrible! I mean I won't shake hands with anybody from San Francisco." - Richard Nixon, quoted during the Watergate Tapes sometime in 1973.

Researchers and critics are quick to point out that the origins of Bohemian Grove may lie in the ancient Druidic circles of the Celts or the Eleusinian mysteries of the Greeks; exclusive, typically all-male, rites in which celebrants huddled around a bonfire beneath starlit nights, sharing communal mysteries of death and rebirth through the sacrifice of a bull in homage to the gods. But the truth of the Grove's origin is much more mundane—if no less romantic, in a distinctly American way.

Bohemian Grove emerged from a private but informal club of artists, journalists and writers known as the Bohemian Club. The original Bohemian Club was founded in 1872 by a group of journalists who sought to foster a mutual appreciation of the arts and pursued a romantic if hackneyed notion of the artist as a poverty-stricken garrett dweller devoted more to his chosen medium than the mundanities of daily life (although Oscar Wilde was noted to have remarked upon visiting the Club in 1882, "*I never saw so many well-dressed, well-fed, business-looking Bohemians in my life.*") There's always been a long-running pretension of artistic patronage among political figures (perhaps as true today as it was in the 19th century) enamored with the myth of the starving artist, and it soon became apparent that the meager salaries of a journalist could be easily bought by both political and industrial funding. The result being that by the turn of the century, the likes of Ambrose Bierce and composer Louis Glass were hobnobbing regularly with the likes of Henry Morgan and William Randolph Hearst.

Eventually by the 1940s, owing to frequent visits by such prominent entities as Presidents Herbert Hoover and Calvin Coolidge, artists represented only a minute fraction of the Grove's regular visitors, with Senators, bankers and prominent diplomats soon came to dominate the booze-soaked discourse and atmosphere. Alliances of global significance were forged; plans were laid; and plots were hatched that came to designate Bohemian Grove as less a relaxing weekend getaway as some of the most significant blueprints for social engineering as we know it.

In 1929, a 40 foot statue of an owl, sculpted by noted Armenian-American sculptor (and Grove president) Haig Patigian, came to serve as a central focus of Bohemian Grove and has been associated as the most visible emblem of this secretive clique ever since. Most notably, it serves as the backdrop for the Grove's climactic "Cremation of Care" ceremony, a dramatization intended to symbolize the sacrifice of the cares, anxieties and worries of day to day existence (presumably, only of those affecting beleaguered servants of international finance.) The rite has since been enhanced by advanced electronics and pyrotechnic displays and, most dramatically for many years, the stentorian voice of Grove member Walter Cronkite; with leaked video footage giving the impression of something between a pagan ritual, an elaborate high school drama production and a laser light show (one quote regarding the Grove's penchant for dramatics has been noted as stating that there are far more cost effective ways to waste energy budgets than on a fraternity talent show; but then again, the average American's tax dollars are typically spent in any number of irrelevant ways and that politicians need creative expense budgets as much as anyone else.)

It's worth noting here that the owl has a myriad of different meanings from culture to culture. While for the Greeks, the bird was most strongly associated with the figure of Athena, goddess of wisdom and learning, for cultures including the Egyptians and the Celts, the owl represented the underworld; the overseer of souls through the subterranean hallways of death. And given that many of the top players over the years at Bohemian Grove have been linked to not only the shadowy echelons of power and control but assassination and wholesale murders under the guise of national wars and elaborately pre-staged "accidents," it is perhaps more fitting that this latter symbolism be kept in mind.

Of somewhat curious interest are the 'encampments' (a term sometimes found in Masonic and Masonic-derived circles in reference to a gathering of Masons) found at Bohemian Grove. These are primarily patrilineal quarters assigned to participants based on their particular status or field of industry, typically assigned with a self-effacing or jovial nickname;

for example, the "Hill Billy Camp" is assigned to banking, political or media figures (typically with a net worth in excess of $15 Million). Others have included the Owl's Nest (for presidents and military/defense contractors); Lost Angels (banking and defense Contractors); Cave Man (education and think-tanks, as well as oil companies and the media); Uplifters (corporate executives); Stowaway (oil companies, big business and Rockefellers); Silverado squatters (big business and defense contractors); Hideaway (think tanks and military/defense contractors); and Sempervirens (California corporations). It is in these encampments (in 2007, there were some 118) that contacts are forged and plans laid in the musk of the cabins reeking of 18-year old single malt Scotch and smug vainglory.

It is presumably in one of these very cabins in July of 1942 that plans were initially hatched between Dr. Ernest Lawrence, Dr. Robert Oppenheimer and the Hungarian-born Edward Teller, as well as various military and defense officials that would eventually lead to the Manhattan Project; an undertaking costing in excess of $2 billion dollars that led to the development of the Atomic bomb. Grove members are understandably proud of an achievement that cost the death of over 135,000 individuals—the vast majority, innocent civilians—and rarely miss a chance to regale newcomers to the festivities with countless tales heard second, third, fourth, and fifth-hand about what really went on beneath the whispering of the pines when Standard Oil money met U.C. Berkeley hands to fund the decisive American victory of WWII.

It should be noted that the Grove even has their own patron saint in the form of St. John of Nepomuk, a martyred fourteenth century saint who was tortured and drowned by the Bohemian King Wenceslaus in the Vltava River rather than reveal the confessional secrets of the Bohemian Queen. Grove members claim that the figurehead represents the vow of secrecy that each member is sworn to uphold. Yet in light of the figure's symbolic placement directly overlooking the Russian River, one wonders if it serves as a warning to would-be trespassers of the fate that may occur should they accidentally spill on to the secrets of the Grove.

Controversy of Bohemian Grove

It should here be noted that no official deaths or accidents have ever been noted in conjunction with the Grove's almost 150-year existence. Infiltrators have gone on to publish, document and videotape accounts of the on-goings without censure; presumably other than the embarrassment suffered by grown men—the supposed exemplars of cultural and moral prestige—drunkenly cavorting in front of a 40 foot effigy of an owl while the fate of the western world hangs in the hand of their junior executors. Still, not only is the correlation between Bohemian Grove and numerous other, much less frivolous, cliques well documented, on-goings at the Grove still carry the stigma of numerous unanswered questions.

As mentioned earlier, one of the central 'rites' of Bohemian Grove is the ceremony known as the Cremation of Care, which invokes the figure of Bacchus—e.g., the Greek Dionysus, god of divine intoxication, ecstasy and vision—as patron of the Grove to rise from beyond the dead (it is interesting to note that 'Grove' itself is a term used by adherents of the modern Witchcraft movement, also as a court of 'learning' with 'inner groves' reserved only for the elect initiates of a coven). This seems parallel to the central plot of the *Bacchae* of Euripides, written in the fifth century B.C. where the god, enslaved and imprisoned by King Pentheus, Lord of Thebes, escapes and, disguised himself as a foreigner, leads his band of female Maenads in rites of sexual licentiousness and frenzy, eventually resulting in the sacrifice of Pentheus. Keep in mind that the celebrating Maenads are exclusively female; the participants of Bohemian Grove, on the other hand, are of course exclusively male. A quote from author and noted Grove member Herman Wouk springs to mind here: *"Men can decently love each other; they always have, but women never quite understand."*

But a more serious charge has emerged surrounding the club since the 1980s; that of many Grove member's predilections for prostitution, particular of an excessively seedy kind. Sex workers—and it is worth noting, both female *and* male—have told allegations (perhaps graciously, perhaps fearfully, refusing to name names in all but a few cases) of lavish S & M-themed gatherings in the outer reaches of the camp that involved forced degradation, humiliation and forced injury (according to one former escort, by a circle consisting of several former Republican secretaries of state and defense) which left them scarred permanently and afraid for their lives. The Grove, however, as a non-profit private institution is outside the jurisdiction of state criminal investigation presumably *because* of the very influence it wields.

Insinuations of sexual deviancy are one thing. Evidence of the influence of the Grove—particularly in nominally conservative, right-leaning Republican circles, from whom the Grove draws its strongest constituency—is apparent throughout American history. In his memoirs, former President (and Freemason) Herbert Hoover states that after then-President Calvin Coolidge's announcement that he would not run for a second term in 1927, "*a hundred men... editors, publishers, public officials and others from all over the country who were at the Grove, came to my camp demanding that I announce my candidacy.*" The following summer, the Republican party unanimously supported Hoover's bid for presidency, a tenure which saw the development of the Council on Foreign Relations directly under his oversight. And indeed, membership at the Grove seems to have been a preliminary requisite for just about every Republican president since the foundation of the clique since Hoover; most notably, the candidacies of Nixon, Reagan and both George H.W. and George W. Bush are alleged to have found their initial support within the clustered encampments of Bohemian Grove, and more recently, California governor Arnold Schwarzenegger's entry into the fray of state politics was secured by a raucous crowd of supporters from various encampments.

Nor is Bohemian Grove a strictly American phenomenon. In 1991, the Grove elected as one of its keynote speakers former German Chancellor Helmut Schmidt. Schmidt, a public and unapologetic member of the Council on Foreign Relations, the Trilateral Commission and enthusiastic participant in the Bilderberg conferences, sparked controversy in the 1960s and 70s when it was revealed that he was a former member of the Nazi Hitler Youth party (and interestingly enough, adding to the Luciferian spectre of Bohemian Grove, Schmidt's wife's nickname is "Loki; the same name as the mythological deity equated to Satan in Germanic mythology.) What makes this association all the more curious are reports in the 1970s that one regular Grove attendee was a charming but unrepentant former Nazi who drove around in a jeep that had a decal of Rommel's campaign to Africa affixed to its bumper—a palm tree surmounted by a swastika. Rumor has it that then-President Gerald Ford, in an uncharacteristic move of common sense, forced the gentleman to remove the offending bumper sticker.

Not surprisingly, wherever the threat of exclusivity and secrecy raises its head, the last name Rockefeller appears; and Bohemian Grove is certainly no exception. Since the 1920s, the Rockefeller family have been long-standing contributors to the atmosphere of the Grove gatherings, and the names of both directors and junior level members of Rockefeller-derived institutions and foundations remain some of the Grove's most cherished key players. Yet the Rockefeller family isn't the only family to come up in conjunction as a bridge between Bohemian Grove and prominent families in the Illuminati. For many years, John E. DuPont III was a regular attendee, and was even invited *after* his 1997 conviction of first degree murder; including up to and after his 2010 death (an oversight or a deliberate example of Grove organizer's morbid sense of humor?)

The figure of Henry Kissinger is perhaps one of the most notorious and venerable old guards of the Grove, and one which has been known to enjoy certain "executive privileges" on the grounds, the details of which are best left to the imagination of the reader. Nor has this connection been a relatively more recent occurrence; as far back as 1905, Bohemian Grove's honorary president was one Daniel Coit Gilman, both a Freemason and founder of the Russell Trust Association, the official trustees of the Skull & Bones Society of Chapter Seven. Gaylord Freeman, both the most prominent member of the Freeman bloodline of the Illuminati explored in Chapter Three as well as alleged head of the Priory of Sion, was a regular attendee starting in the late 30s. James Wolfensohn, former president of the World Bank Group and close ally of the Rothschild dynasty (whom, when once asked about the downside of globalization, was quoted as saying, *"With all the forces making our world smaller, it is time to change our way of thinking, to realize we live in one world and not many different worlds"*) is another figure who has been known to enjoy a certain carte blanche at the tables of Bohemian Grove.

Stephen Bechtel, the octogenarian heir to the Bechtel Corporation (a civil engineering firm specializing in nuclear power and having almost exclusive ties to Rothschild funded projects and think tanks) is another grand old guard legacy member—one who has been known to perform in various skits organized by Bohemian Grove officers in full drag, alongside such venerable figures of republican politics as Caspar Weinberger and James Baker.

Dangers of Bohemian Grove

When all is said and done, it's easy for the rational, incredulous observer to dismiss many of the more creative implications of the Bohemian Grove phenomenon—say, an annual gathering of reptilian overlords involved in international human sacrifice trafficking trades—as nothing more than a rather convoluted flight of fancy. But it's even more easy to throw the proverbial baby out with the bathwater and casually dismiss Bohemian Grove as a mere "boys only" beer blowout backed by bizarre and elaborate scenery and an obscene display of personal wealth and arrogance. The alleged Satanism of Bohemian Grove, if it exists at all, is but a mere metaphor for the blood-laden trail left behind by greed, omniscient authority and globalization. Its cultists are hardly hooded diabolists out of a poorly scripted horror film, but the same power-brokers and puppet masters who have served avarice in all its twisted forms. *Wherever two or more are gathered together in my name, I am there in the midst.* This quote, from Matthew 18:20, is as accurate for the hordes of the world elite as it is for ostensibly any question. Only, the god of the elite is neither Christ, Jehovah, Allah or even Lucifer. It's name is Mammon, and its legions are indeed, many.

Members

Membership in Bohemian Grove was once thought to be a purely exclusive phenomenon, guarded under lock and key; one whose divulging would result in the strictest penalty, be it of death or worse. These days, current research indicates this is far from the case. Members outside the parties referred to previously in this chapter have included: former Speaker of the House Newt Gingrich; former Vice President (and Council on Foreign Relations advisor) Dick Cheney; conservative pundit William F. Buckley, Jr.; Coldwell Banker founder Colbert Coldwell; former Southern Pacific President Alan Furth; billionaires Paul and Charles Koch; TV host Art Linkletter; actor Clint Eastwood; former teen idol Fabian; economist (and Committee of 300 member) George Soros; former Motorola CEO Robert Galvin; Senator Lamar Alexander; former Secretary of State (and Council on Foreign Relations advisor) Colin Powell; former Secretary of Defense (and Council on Foreign Relations member) Evan

Galbraith; former Secretary of State (and Trilateral Commission member) George Shultz; Hilton CEO Barron Hilton I; former Singapore Prime Minister Lee Kuan Yew; former Attorney General Ed Meese; Hewlett-Packard founder David Packard; Draper International founder William Henry Draper; former General Norman Schwarzkopf; Nixon Secretary of Defense Robert McNamara; former Secretary of State (and Bilderberg attendee) Warren Christopher; presidential advisor (and Trilateral Commission member) David Gergen; former Secretary of Defense Donald Rumsfeld; former Coors president Joseph Coors; Congressman David Dreier; former Federal Reserve Chairman Alan Greenspan; former Rockwell CEO Donald Beall; entertainment mogul Merv Griffin; Boeing director Harold Haynes; Ford chairman Carl Reichardt; Gulf & Western director Judd Leighton; former Monsanto CEO Richard Mahoney; McDonald's founder Ray Kroc; former Naval Secretary (and member of the 9/11 Commission) John F. Lehman; Federal Judge Charles A. Legge; entrepreneur and publisher Malcolm Forbes; Mississippi Governor Haley Barbour; former Chief Justice Earl Warren; former Federal Prosecutor Kenneth Starr; and Supreme Court Justice Antonin Scalia.

Chapter Ten: THE SOCIETY OF JESUITS

In the dimly lit caverns of secret societies, no institution seems more out of place than the Society of Jesus—or more popularly known, the Jesuits. With a global population of some 18,000 adherents, the Jesuit Order are one of the most visible and well-known defenders of the Roman-Catholic faith in the world today. Reknown for their educational institutions (Jesuit schools have consistently ranked among the top tier of U.S. colleges and universities) and the stringency of their seminaries, the Jesuits seem more like a throwback to the theological standards of the 18th and 19th centuries rather than a monolithic beast with its eye on the goal of global domination—particularly in the face of what both theologians and non-religious commenters have noted to be an increasingly secularized world.

Yet while the Jesuit Society may not be the sole religious society alone in maintaining some damning secrets, secrecy is at the core of Jesuit history. Like the larger Catholic faith, Jesuits have been plagued by recent sex scandals occurring both in the U.S. and abroad. In 2011, the regional province of the Society of Jesus in the Pacific Northwest was ordered to pay a fine totaling $166 million to some 450 survivors—many of them Native American—of sexual abuse as children from Jesuit priests over a total of some fifty years. While the recently elected Pope Francis (already dubbed "the Pope of the people)—himself, noted as the first Jesuit pope—has vowed to mercilessly investigate and prosecute clergy accused of abuse, his top prosecutor in the Vatican (a Jesuit, as well) was recently implicated as being one of several Catholic officials responsible for continuing to allow a Chicago priest with a long history of similar allegations to remain in ministry.

As damning as these scandals may be (and it needs to be stated that rumors of sexual abuse within the Catholic church are from a wholly modern occurrence, but has been alleged for well over a hundred years now), there may be more that the Jesuits may need to answer for than charges of sexual molestation and rape, as horrific as they are. As mentioned earlier in Chapter Three, the historical origins of the Illuminati can be seen largely as a response to the prevailing Jesuit influence in education, dating as far back as the 18th century. Yet, there is another more modern, even more sinister confluence arising as a reaction to Jesuit influence; Heinrich Himmler's elite SS force of the Nazi Party, modeled directly on the military ethos of the Jesuits yet designed to combat the threat of Catholicism and its various offshoots (which, in 1939, accounted for approximately 40% of German people.) But beyond this lurks an even more subterranean duplicity ascribed to the Jesuits; and it is this strand and its maneuverings into the worlds of secret society and hidden influence that allows for a final chapter for much of what we have been discussing to date.

Origins of the Society of Jesuits

The Society of Jesus was founded by St. Ignatius of Loyola, a Spanish knight who had been wounded during the Battle of Pamplona in 1521 and subsequently experienced a religious conversion, later recounted in his famed *Spiritual Exercises* (to this day, still considered a fundamental classic of spiritual literature.) In 1534, Ignatius and six other pilgrims announced the formation of the Society of Jesus, professing vows of poverty, asceticism, chastity and strict and absolute obedience to the rule of the Pope and the Holy See.

Ignatius' military background culminated in a stringent, chivalric spiritual knighthood where members were vowed to accept orders from the church wherever in the world they may live, often under the most extreme conditions imaginable. This martial attitude of absolute devotion to the Society and to the Vatican enabled the Jesuits' colloquial appellate of being "God's Soldiers" and "the Secret Service of the Vatican", earning them a strong reputation for their roles in the Counter Reformation and the Spanish Inquisition of the 17th century and eventually the implementation of the Second Vatican Council of 1962, otherwise known as Vatican II, which implicitly modernized the Catholic Church by allowing the recitation of the Mass in English, among other more contemporary developments.

Early Jesuit growth was established through a long scale period of missionary conversion, particularly in developing countries among indigenous peoples, resulting from Spanish explorations of the New World in North and South America in the 17th and 18th centuries. Critical to this growth was the need for a common enemy, and the newly emerged Protestant faith found itself at increasing odds with the rabidly zealous Jesuits.

Resultantly, an edict of formal suppression of the Jesuits under strong secular pressure was signed by Pope Clement XIV in July of 1773 (a full three years before the founding of the Illuminati), a suppression that would affect all of Europe with the exception of Prussia (which included both Poland and Bavaria due to the empire's growth at the time) and Russia. It is through these particular kingdoms that the work of the Jesuits was able to continue unabated despite formal suppression; and coincidentally, both these kingdoms saw a distinct rise in both Masonic and Masonically derived bodies during that same time. The suppression was officially reversed by the bull of Pope Pius VII in 1814, subsequent to the Napoleonic wars (wars, it should be noted, that were directly financed by the now-familiar Rothschild bloodline of the Illuminati. Also worth taking into consideration is Napoleon's own role as a historic Freemason and Illuminati member.)

The role of the Napoleonic wars should be examined in light of the emperor's relation to the Illuminati and Freemasonry. The conflicts and Napoleonic territorial expansion helped pave the way for continued Illuminati conquest, with both the church and its constituents under frequent target as being representatives of the "old" order which both Napoleon and the Illuminati sought to overthrow. In particular, Pope Pius VII under increasingly strained relations with Napoleon; relations which resulted in his exile in the Italian seaport of Savona after French conquest and annex of the Papal States in 1809. Pius's release was eventually guaranteed by the defeat of Napoleon at Waterloo in 1815 and the subsequent Congress of Vienna, and both Jesuit restoration and return to papal rule was declared throughout many formerly Catholic provinces of Europe.

Yet both Pius and church had found themselves in an increasingly changed world after the 12 years of fighting and revolution the wars had wrought across Europe. No longer was Catholicism the predominate Christian faith; its assured *bete noire* of Protestantism has supplanted its iron hold throughout much of Europe, with the result that the papacy was forced to adapt to the changes of increasing egalitarianism and colonization that was changing both the geographic and cultural outlook of European thought. The result was the increased visibility of Jesuit presence in the still burgeoning United States, particularly in educational institutions. The establishment and domination of almost all of the 28 Jesuit colleges and universities occurred immediately following the restoration of Jesuit expansion by Pius, resulting in adherence to a strict orthodoxy and doctrine of papal infallibility that up until relatively recent times immediately preceding the Second Vatican Council of 1962 (itself, an effort on behalf of the Church to adapt to an increasingly modern and all-inclusive cultural milieu.)

Despite the fact that the Jesuits represent the largest single religious order of priests and clergy within the Catholic church and the continued prominence of Jesuit colleges, the order itself has been experiencing a steady decline over the past forty years owing to the increased popularity of liberation theology (particularly in third world countries), which emphasizes the need for clergy to maintain an express awareness to the plight of the impoverished and directly redress social injustice as an adjunct to the mission of the church. Critics have referred to this as a form of Marxist Christianity, and even espy an evidence of Illuminati doctrine in its philosophical underpinnings. But criticism of the Jesuits isn't wholly a modern phenomenon owing to the advent of economic dilemmas of poverty and wealth distribution. Nor does it stem back to the rise of Protestantism. The criticism of the Jesuit faith is not rooted in their ideology but in their actions. And it's been documented as early as the 17th century.

Controversy of the Society of Jesuits

The earliest criticism of the Jesuits was published in 1612 as the *Monita Secreta Iesutus* or *Secret Instructions of the Jesuits*. Now widely considered a hoax attributed to a former Brother named Jerome Zahorowski who had been excommunicated a year earlier, the book purports to be the secret instructions of the society's fifth grandmaster Claudio Acquaviva and alleges, among other things, that Jesuit clergy must acquire wealth for the Society by any means imaginable including enticing wealthy men to enter it and will the society their estates; convincing rich widows to endow their assets to the Society and dissuading them from remarriage; and the wholesale slander of other monastic orders. While now discredited both by the church and its detractors, the criticism does raise a fundamental question; just how was a monastic and military-styled order sworn to poverty and renunciation able to forge a niche of such commendable power within the ranks of the church that by the time of the Counter Reformation (initiated some mere ten years after the Society's official founding) they numbered among the most revered, most popular and most revered orders within the Roman Catholic church?

Intriguingly enough, it wasn't until the rise of the Enlightenment in the 18th century—which, as Chapter Three and Chapter Four demonstrated, was in no small part a result of Masonic and Illuminati influence—that Jesuit conspiracies began to be more widespread. Conflicts between Catholicism and Freemasonry had been festering for numerous years prior; and indeed, to this date, there is a mutual enmity between the Vatican and the vast majority of Masonic lodges. Accusations of Jesuit support was a popular rebuttal to church-abetted attacks on the rationalism of Rousseau and Voltaire; and the term "Jesuit" became an increasingly derogatory epithet well into the 19th century, when anti-clericism became a common facet of French intellectual life, thanks to such writers as famed French historian and 'philosopher of pessimism' Jules Michelet. Conversely, Jesuit supporters had a ready counter-argument in their own nemesis of Adam Weishaupt but by then, it was too late; Masonic and Illuminati ideals had come into their own rarely-waning vogue both in the New World and the old.

Yet, much like other secret societies—as well as the Catholic church itself—the Jesuits maintain their own secretive rites of induction. After all, what is a military order without some sense of pageantry, some sense of formal ritual decorum, that defies the rational and instead reminds the candidate that he is no longer invested with mortal indenture but instead serves a higher calling? This is as true for the Marine as it is for the Freemason; and subsequently, the Jesuit.

One account states that a Jesuit called to the rank of command swears an oath of fealty not to God or to the betterment of mankind, but to the direct authority of the Pope, whom is viewed as the mortal representative of the Lord on Earth. He does so beneath two banners: one being a banner bearing the official papal colors, the other a black banner emblazoned with the image of a dagger and a skull and crossbones (a curious image, given Chapter Seven.) Directly above this image is the legend INRI, often found on images of the crucifix and generally held to be shorthand for the Latin *Iesus Nazarenus, Rex Iudaeorum* or "Jesus of Nazareth, King of the Jews." However, this account states that the legend is actually shorthand for *Iustum Necar, Reges*

Impious or Latin for "It is just to murder an impious king" (it is interesting to compare this legend with the hermetic and qabalistic practice of *notariqon*, whereby the acronym of a popular phrase is held to have numerous mystical meanings to be discovered through a complex numerological analysis.)

This same account goes on to quote the "Extreme Oath of the Jesuits" which states, among other things, that the candidate is sworn to "*plant the seeds of jealousy and hatred between communities, provinces, states that were at peace, and incite them to deeds of blood, involving them in war with each other, and to create revolutions and civil wars in countries that were independent and prosperous, cultivating the arts and the sciences and enjoying the blessings of peace. To take sides with the combatants and to act secretly with your brother Jesuit, who might be engaged on the other side, but openly opposed to that with which you might be connected, only that the Church might be the gainer in the end, in the conditions fixed in the treaties for peace and that the end justifies the means.*"

At the conclusion of this oath, the candidate is questioned through a series of direct interrogations regarding his motivations and his obligations that is strikingly reminiscent of Masonic oaths (perhaps the latter being a perversion of pre-existing Jesuit obligations?) including being received by a mysterious *"venerable man with white hair"* (itself, reminiscent of the Templar oath to Baphomet), and concludes with the charge, *"Go ye, then, into all the world and take possession of all lands in the name of the Pope. He who will not accept him as the Vicar of Jesus and his Vice-regent on earth, let him be accursed and exterminated."*

The Catholic Church and the CIA have long enjoyed a mutually respectful relationship; and some say, a mutual vying for power. This relationship dates all the way back to the 1940s in the midst of WWII when General William Donovan, then head of the Office of Strategic Services (the precursor of the CIA), was received by Pope Pius XII to be granted the Grand Cross of the Order of Saint Sylvester, the oldest and most prestigious of papal knighthoods, on accounts of his alliance with the Catholic intelligence service Pro Deo.

Since then, the links between the CIA and the Vatican have been marked by a pronounced, if at times competitive, alliance, particularly in regions such as Latin America and Eastern Europe where Catholicism has garnered an unwavering popularity, especially in the face of documented CIA activity during the 1970s and 1980s. Both Vatican funding of covert CIA operations as well as CIA sponsorship of the traditionalist "Opus Dei" movement, which helped infiltrate and combat Communist sympathies during the Cold War, has been ably documented; and the relationship between the Vatican and Licio Gelli's Masonic "Propaganda Due" lodge has been linked to discretionary CIA funding, with a number of unanswered questions regarding Gelli's dismissed criminal charges and CIA involvement still lingers for many.

Former CIA director William Casey as well as his close colleague, former Secretary of State Alexander Haig, were both noted members of the Knights of Malta, a Jesuit-allied military order who also were responsible for the smuggling of thousands of Nazi war criminals into South America immediately following WWII through Catholic Bishop Alois Hudal's "underground railroad", including noted Jesuit father Martin Bormann (despite the fact that Jesuits were a frequent target for Gestapo persecution in WWII, this appears only on account of Catholicism's popularity in Germany at the time.

The truth of the matter is that the Nazis openly cooperated with the Vatican, and by default Jesuits, as documented evidence has proven time and time again. Benito Mussolini, the Fascist Italian dictator and close ally of Hitler, as well as the openly-Fascist admirant and Nazi criminal harborer Argentinian President Juan Peron.) Other members of the Knights of Malta have included Nixon-era CIA Director William Colby, Lee Iacocca, William F. Buckley, Pat Buchanan, J. Patrick Grace, Cold War-era CIA Director John A. McCone and Cardinal John Joseph O'Connor; all of whom have had noted ties to the Council on Foreign Relations.

Certainly, adherence to the Jesuit faith does not imply nefarious or conspiratorial intent anymore than adherence to Catholicism implies pedophilia or Nazi war crime-support. But it is curious how a supposedly secular (and some would argue Masonically-derived) nation such as America and an allegedly secular (and unquestionably unethical) nation such as that of Nazi Germany could openly cooperate with the Vatican , and by default, their own "Secret Service", the Society of Jesuits? Unless there was another, perhaps "hidden", mechanism at hand...

That mechanism will be better left for the more astute reader to ascertain.

Members

Other members of the Society of Jesuits and allied Vatican organizations have included: Mathematician (and peer of Galileo) Luca Valerio; St. Francis Xavier; author Garry Wills; former Senator Frank Lausche (Knight of Malta); political pundit John McLaughlin; Prince Laurent of Belgium (Knight of Malta); controversial author Father Malachi Martin; Belgian physicist Georges LeMaitre; French Minister of Defense Patrick Levaye (Knight of Malta); Hitler biographer Franz Jetzinger; linguist Peter Hans Kolvenbach; scientist, mystic and discoverer of microbes Athanasius Kircher; writer Augustin Barruel; former German Chancellor Franz von Papen (Knight of Malta); philosopher Yves Marie Andre; philosopher Joseph de Maistre; Cardinal Avery Dulles; King Juan Carlos I of Spain (Knight of Malta); former Congressman Robert Drinan; physicist and astronomer Francesco Maria Grimaldi; philosopher Baltasar Gracian; Crown Prince Otto von Habsburg (Knight of Malta); author John Powell; Congressman Gabriel Richard; poet Gerald Manley Hopkins; Bloomingdale's founder

Alfred Bloomingdale (Knight of Malta); philosopher Martin Heidegger; explorer Simon le Moyne; philosopher Pierre Teilhard de Chardin; former CIA Counterintelligence Chief James Angleton (Knight of Malta); Gregorian calendar architect Christopher Clavius; former Secretary of the Interior Walter Hickel (Knight of Malta); labor activist John Corridan; scientist Louis Bernard Castel; author James Martin; mathematician Andres Tacquet; former Senator Rick Santorum (Knight of Malta); Belgian political leader and SS officer Leon Degrelle; artist Andreas Pozzo; former Inspector General of the Department of Defense Joseph Schmitz (Knight of Malta); poet Robert Southwell; and former U.S. Secretary of Energy James D. Watkins (Knight of Malta).

Afterword

It's been almost a thousand years since Hassan-i-Sabbah first oversaw his elite cadre of highly trained and highly indoctrinated *Hashishin* from his mountain fortress at Alamut, inaugurating a dynastic reign of terror that lasted less than only two hundred years. And it's been almost 250 years since the mercurial presence of Adam Weishaupt flickered in and out of seminaries and secretive candle-lit lodges to inaugurate what may be the world's longest concurrently running shaggy dog story, or such a substantial threat to global freedom that the human mind would prefer to keep its head in the sand rather than address its ramifications. Since that time, the world has been baptized both in blood and peace time and time again; seen the establishment of new nations, new ideologies, new faiths, world wars and the development of weapons and diseases that could potentially spell the demise of existence of the human race as we know it; and at the crux of each cataclysm, names occur and reoccur in strange and mysterious configurations, a cuneiform that only time and dedicated research can decipher.

It's been said that when Swiss psychologist Carl Jung first read James Joyce's virtually impenetrable and nonsensical *Finnegan's Wake*, he commented that *"this is either an example of severe mental illness or a degree of mental health inconceivable to most people."* And for millions of people, the analogy can be extended to the idea of secret societies; either they are a fertile example of the paranoid human imagination to distort and skew coincidence to an absurd degree, or they are a byproduct of the human imagination's ability to distort, skew and control human society to a degree unfathomable to paranoia and absurdity. Time and time again, names, events and occurrences occur in such close proximity to one another to make the factor of coincidence a virtual improbability; and time and time again, the average person ascribes to these confluences the magical property of "coincidence", demonizing believers as paranoid cranks and gullible swallowers of a dissociative brand of snake oil.

There's no doubt that some of the more fanciful descriptions of these societies are no doubt figments of the author's imagination, and highly profitable figments at that. But beyond the inane absurdity of certain allegations (the notion of a dynasty of shape-shifting reptilian/human hybrids responsible for the infiltration of every conceivable social mechanism since time immemorial instantly comes to mind), the very real question when faced with the plausibility of detailing secret societies is best summed up by the question, who gains? The author, who faces the distinct probability of a lifetime of ostracism, ridicule and marginalization for daring to 'suggest' that there may be figures who stand to gain and historically *have* gained by the non-judicious exercise of control, nepotism and influence and who have perpetuated a far-reaching vision and schematic of that control and are willing to sacrifice the lives of others to ensure that control remains forever cemented? The architects of that control, whose movements are forever under scrutiny being public figures who continue to exist in an age of diminished privacy? The subjects of that control, who knowingly or unknowingly trade personal liberty and freedom of both thought and expression in exchange for an illusion of security? Or the unseen hand which, by its very inconspicuousness, gains profit and power in full public purview according to the age-old designs of greed and authority?

I am often asked whether or not I take the subject of secret societies with a grain of salt. I typically answer no; but it's likely that they take *me* with a grain of salt. What I mean by that, is that despite the threat of public exposure from numerous sides, both as often politically or religiously non-sectarian as they are sectarian, these same architects of control and domination continue to act with impunity, fulfilling designs as brazenly and predictably as any poorly scripted Hollywood thriller. It's not that I believe they are oblivious to criticism or exposure; it's just that I believe they have become so adroitly capable of mastering misinformation and miscommunication that even criticism, exposure and widespread public outcry can be easily skewed and twisted so as to be grafted on to their schemes to suit their best interests.

As I mentioned earlier in the introduction, the notion of secret societies is no longer a distinctly underground phenomenon; but then again it never *has* been. Not only have many so-called "shadow" organizations operated out in the open, but warnings as to their threats have appeared since at least the 18th century. What has changed is public perception of these threats. The secret society is now enjoying a semi-ironic prestige in popular culture, with numerous movies, novels, musicians and internet sites celebrating (often smugly and frequently superficially) the lore of these entities with all the free abandon and self-conscious winking and nudging one has come to expect in the digital age. I say, "semi-ironically" because these same purveyors of Illuminati chic seem to play right into the ploys and designs of those power barons they choose to blithely dismiss as nothing more than a fashion statement.

At the opposite end of the spectrum, the explosion in popularity of the subject has fostered a plethora of books; some meticulously researched, some novel and some fundamentally prejudiced. Which has led to a great question: if these organizations are so powerful, why aren't the authors of these exposes dead yet? The answer is simple; the most critical way to deflect your opponent's arguments is to denigrate them. Silencing your opponent won't stifle his or her argument; but by deriding that argument, you make it known (through a somewhat curious twist of logic) that disagreement with your own is nothing more than a cause for public humiliation. And public humiliation is par for the course for these organizations.

My personal stance on the subject matter is that there are, indeed, elements beyond our conscious control which seek to manipulate information and public opinion to best serve the needs of an authority which seeks to consolidate power through the process of globalization and the direct silencing of dissenting opinions. As to the motivation behind these entities, I don't believe that they are necessarily exclusive to one particular political, cultural or religious ideology, but are much more abstract in their outlook, seeking power for its own sake. My personal opinion is that we are currently living in a world where freedom of expression and livelihood are being threatened by these very entities, and it is the distinct duty of anyone possessed with the slightest semblance of conscience to combat these entities by any and every means necessary.

I don't pretend that this is either the first or the last book to be written on the subject. I don't pretend that somewhere down the line, a much abler researcher will not compose a work that will not only be much more resolutely documented, but will provide irrevocable evidence for the existence of these societies and the dangers they pose to the very foundations of the world as we know it. Not only do I not pretend this, I actively hope and welcome it. The wool can only be pulled over the eyes for so long until somebody wakes up. The lie may seduce sweetly for now, but its neck will eventually be pierced by truth. And like freedom, the truth, as

much wiser men have noted, is a two-edged
sword.

Made in the USA
Middletown, DE
30 June 2018